SAUL BELLOW

In the same series:

BERTOLT BRECHT   *Willy Haas*
ALBERT CAMUS   *Carol Petersen*
T. S. ELIOT   *Joachim Seyppel*
WILLIAM FAULKNER   *Joachim Seyppel*
MAX FRISCH   *Carol Petersen*
MAKSIM GORKI   *Gerhard Habermann*
GÜNTER GRASS   *Kurt Lothar Tank*
HERMANN HESSE   *Franz Baumer*
JAMES JOYCE   *Armin Arnold*
FRANZ KAFKA   *Franz Baumer*
THOMAS MANN   *Arnold Bauer*
EUGENE O'NEILL   *Horst Frenz*
EZRA POUND   *Jeannette Lander*
JEAN-PAUL SARTRE   *Liselotte Richter*
ISAAC BASHEVIS SINGER   *Irving Malin*
THORNTON WILDER   *Hermann Stresau*

Modern Literature Monographs

SAUL BELLOW

Brigitte Scheer-Schäzler

Frederick Ungar Publishing Co.
New York

For
Rudolf Scheer
my husband
whose goodness is no metaphor

Acknowledgments

I should like to express my sincere thanks to several persons who have kindly and generously supported my writing this book: to Dr. Richard W. Downar, Director of the American Studies Program of the American Council of Learned Societies, and to the ACLS itself for the grant that enabled me to study in the United States; to my dear friend Elaine Barry of Monash University, Melbourne, to whom I shall always be indebted for her painstaking corrections of the manuscript and her invaluable suggestions for improvements; to Miss Maureen Lindsay of Rutgers University for her enlightening comments on the first draft; and, most of all, to Lina Mainiero of Frederick Ungar Publishing Company without whose understanding and encouragement this book could not have taken shape.

Contents

	Chronology	ix
	Introduction	1
1	*The Price of Release*	7
2	*Bitterness in His Chosen Thing*	31
3	*The Dread Is Great, The Soul Is Small*	59
4	*Every Guy Has His Own Africa*	77
5	*History, Memory—That Is What Makes Us Human*	91
6	*The Benefit of an Enlarged Vision*	117
	Notes	129
	Bibliography	139
	Index	144

Chronology

10 July 1915: Born in Lachine, a suburb of Montreal, in the province of Quebec, Canada.

1924: Bellow family moves to Chicago.

1933: Enters the University of Chicago.

1935: Transfers to Northwestern University.

1937: Graduates from Northwestern with honors in anthropology and sociology.

1941: Publishes first short story, "Two Morning Monologues."

1944: Publishes first novel, *Dangling Man*.

1947: Publishes *The Victim*.

1948–50: Travels in Europe, part of the time as Guggenheim Fellow.

1952–53: Creative Writing Fellow at Princeton University.

1953: Publishes *The Adventures of Augie March* (National Book Award for Fiction for first time).

1956: Publishes *Seize the Day*.

1959: Publishes *Henderson the Rain King*.

1960–62: Is editor of the publication *The Noble Savage*.

1964: Publishes *Herzog* (National Book Award for Fiction for second time). *The Last Analysis* has premiere.

1965: Publishes *The Last Analysis*.

1966: Becomes professor at the University of Chicago and

a fellow of the Committee on Social Thought. Is now chairman of the committee.

1968:   Publishes *Mosby's Memoirs* (short stories). Receives the B'nai B'rith Jewish Heritage Award and the Croix de Chevalier des Arts et Lettres.

1970:   Publishes *Mr. Sammler's Planet* (National Book Award for Fiction for third time).

Introduction

Although Saul Bellow and Norman Mailer rarely see eye to eye on matters of life and literature, it is Mailer who has pertinently summed up Bellow's rank and importance: "Saul Bellow," he says, "has the warmest imagination of any writer in my generation."[1] The latest comprehensive study to date, John Clayton's *Saul Bellow: In Defense of Man* reports general consensus among the critics that Saul Bellow is America's most important living novelist.[2] The English critics agree,[3] and the French have devoted a considerable amount of attention to his best-known work, *Herzog*.[4]

Saul Bellow is considered a "contemporary classic."[5] Frequently regarded as heir and successor to William Faulkner, he is believed to be leading the American novel to a summit comparable to that achieved in the 1930s.[6] Nathan Scott correctly rejects the label of "naturalism" for Bellow's work,[7] although there is a strong element of realism, of the every-day concerns, and even of the brutality and ugliness of modern life contained in it. What distinguishes his writing from that of the hard-core naturalists, however, is its multi-dimensional quality. The realism is always skillfully interwoven with fable and fantasy, tempered by irony or laughter at the self caught in the middle of painful struggles. Thus Scott places Bellow in the line that reaches backward from Robert Penn Warren and Faulkner toward Mark Twain and Melville and Hawthorne, and toward the European tradition of Dostoyevsky and Kafka and Sartre.[8]

2

Bellow himself readily acknowledges indebtedness to the American as well as the European tradition. Among writers of particular interest to him, he says, are Dreiser and Whitman, Hemingway, Faulkner, and Fitzgerald, Joyce, Lawrence, and Yeats, and the nineteenth-century Russian writers.[9] He is, however, careful to stress the differences he sees between his own work and intention and much of contemporary American fiction. He rejects nihilism, the psychoanalytic approach, pessimistic Romanticism, the degradation or elimination of the experiencing self, unredeemed black humor, and self-indulgent denigration and hatred of the present and of Western civilization. Neither man nor the novel is doomed. In contrast to many of his contemporaries, Bellow writes in defense of values. He, like all his major characters, is on a quest for them. He affirms, as Clayton says, "the possibility of meaningful individual life in contemporary America,"[10] with the stress placed on possibility.

An often-cited truism indeed holds true of Bellow: it is the varied background that makes an American. Bellow, the youngest of four children, was born in Lachine, Quebec, in 1915, two years after his parents, who were Orthodox Jews, had emigrated from Russia. The family lived in Montreal until 1924, when they moved to Chicago. During his childhood and youth Bellow experienced the pressure of financial struggle, watching his father "fail in a series of enterprises; a bakery, a chain of shops, even handling a contract to make

sacks for the Canadian Government in World War
I."[11] Bellow's father seems to have been inclined toward the adventurous and risky: importing onions
from Egypt into Russia, trading in coal and not in-
suring his trucks.

Bellow's father wanted him to become a doctor
or a lawyer, or a moneymaker, and washed his
hands of him when Bellow declined to pursue any
of these goals. His mother, who was still living
"strictly in the nineteenth century," wanted him to
become a Talmudic scholar in the family tradition.[12] Rejecting his parents' goals, Bellow followed
his own interests at the University of Chicago and
later at Northwestern, from which he graduated in
1937 with honors in anthropology and sociology.
After a few months of graduate study he decided, as
he says, "in my innocence"[13] to become a writer.

He held a job with a W.P.A. writers' project,
preparing pamphlets on American writers. His
first work of fiction, the short story "Two Morning
Monologues," appeared in 1941; his first novel,
Dangling Man, in 1944. Nationwide success came
with *The Adventures of Augie March* (1953), for
which he received the National Book Award. He
has held several teaching jobs at, among others, the
University of Minnesota, Bard College, New York
University, and Princeton University. At present
he is chairman of the Committee on Social
Thought, a select graduate program at the University of Chicago. In addition to frequent traveling
in Europe, he spent most of the years 1948 and

1950 abroad. He has a knowledge of Hebrew and speaks French and Yiddish fluently, a language whose "ironic genius" he greatly values.[14] The three main strands that intertwine in his personality are his Russian heritage, his Jewish upbringing, and his familiarity with the contemporary American scene.

Contemporary America, in particular, supplies the multi-colored, teeming, city background with its endless variety of characters, and the confusion of values that comes to any individual who tries to maintain "at least an idea of himself" amid these pressures. But, more importantly, it also supplies the belief in the freedom of such an individual and in the possibility of improving the human condition.

Bellow demonstrates this conviction by endowing as well as burdening each of his protagonists with the innate knowledge that there is a specific task in each life that no one other than he can do. He is a compassionate author, strongly involved with the lives of the people whom he depicts. To him this participation is a criterion of excellence: "Novels are about others. They lack everything if they lack this sympathetic devotion to the life of someone else."[15] This attitude explains, possibly, his major shortcoming as a novelist: he allows himself to become so absorbed in the minds of his protagonists that his books often lack a convincing, dramatic, effective chain of action. Thus his characters themselves are continually forced to strive for balance and harmony between the inner and the outer world, with the inner always about to win. Bellow never clearly demonstrates how this long-sought state of equilibrium can be realized. However, he more than makes up for this lack in his fictional reality by the wealth of perceptions, recognitions and insights he allows his characters to have, and by the intense, highly personal and exceptionally fluid language in which they render their thoughts. No contemporary American novelist equals Bellow in the precision, wit, and elegance of his style. In relation to himself and in regard to the critical studies of his work, Bellow need not have assured us that "Eros manages somehow to survive analysis; and somehow imagination survives criticism."[16]

1

The Price of Release

Saul Bellow's first novel, *Dangling Man,* was published in 1944 and was preceded only by a few short stories. Like his other two short novels, *The Victim* (1947) and *Seize the Day* (1956), it is precise in its statements, compact in its form and carefully written. Bellow himself describes it as "well-made;"[1] and yet it leaves its reader dissatisfied. It is, quite literally, inconclusive. At the end, the reader has finally joined the protagonist in that it is now he who is left dangling. Joseph, the alienated hero of the story, has been driven to choose between undesirable alternatives—desirable alternatives, as he says, "grow only on imaginary trees."[2] The reader, after having been presented with a mass of evidence, some of which is occasionally contradictory, is left to his own resources to come to terms with Joseph's decision. In this, as well as in other respects, *Dangling Man* foreshadows much of Bellow's later work.

Dangling Man is the diary of twenty-seven-year-old Joseph, whose last name we never learn. The entries cover the period between 15 December 1942, and 9 April 1943, but contain a good deal of thinking back to the times before Joseph felt the compulsion to keep a journal. This urge to write arises from what he calls his "present state of demoralization."[3] Several months before the start of the diary, Joseph, a graduate of the University of Wisconsin, married for five years, had to give up his job at the Inter-American Travel Bureau because of his pending induction in the army. Since Joseph was born in Canada, the induction is being held up by extensive and repetitive bureaucratic maneuvers and Joseph is kept waiting, dangling between two stages of life. Because his call into the army is to be expected any day he cannot find a suitable job and has to live on his wife Iva's earnings. In order to save money they have moved from an apartment to a rooming house that confronts them with much that is unpleasant: noises and smells, little thefts, pettiness, spite, sickness and death. They are also exposed to the accidental glimpses of the trivial as well as the momentous in lives to which they do not relate.

Iva, who works in a library, is not at all reluctant to be the provider. She wants Joseph to enjoy his freedom, to do "all the delightful things," as Joseph rather vaguely puts it, that he will be unable to do in the army.[4] But Joseph becomes "a moral casualty of the war."[5] He turns introspective and self-conscious, then critical of his friends and family, and finally angry at everything and everybody, full of the rage of despair. He uses his journal for the threefold purpose of tracing his development, of putting down his observations from his changed and changing perspective, and of seeking relief from his worries through the act of writing. When the pressures around and

within him become overbearing and seem to
threaten his sanity, Joseph writes to the draft
board requesting his immediate induction. The
last entry celebrates in triumphant shouts the end
of his freedom.

> I am no longer to be held accountable for myself; I am
> grateful for that. I am in other hands, relieved of self-
> determination, freedom canceled.

> Hurray for regular hours!
> And for the supervision of the spirit!
> Long live regimentation![6]

The problem is, of course, not so much one of
the nature of freedom, although there is some discussion of that too, but more of its uses. Joseph
admits that he doesn't know what to do with it.[7]
When he is suddenly halted in his reassuring path
of day-to-day living and confronted with the unknown—in the shape of army life, war, and possible death—he turns back on his past life and past
values and ferociously begins to pluck them all
apart. He has the acute mind that disillusioned
ex-believers of various ideologies sometimes develop. He breaks with his friends of many years,
who now seem to him shallow, cruel, opportunis-
tic and falsely optimistic. He quarrels with his
in-laws, beats his teen-age niece, rejects the help his
older brother Amos offers, and finds Iva increasingly without faith in him. He explodes at the
slightest provocation so that he and Iva are asked
to move from the rooming house. His induction

prevents at least the humiliation this would have meant for Iva.

While Joseph believes that he is extricating himself from deceptive and treacherous bonds he is really giving in to a fast-growing self-centeredness. The demands he makes on people's understanding and compassion outweigh by far the understanding he is willing to give them. He shies away from opportunities to be of help. When he is asked to assist with moving some furniture into the room of a dying old lady, he complies but flees the scene precipitously. He never even considers meeting Iva at the library to take her home, although she works late some nights and is afraid to return alone. Joseph, the great planner, the erector of "ideal constructions" who wished to establish "a 'colony of the spirit,' or a group whose covenants forbade spite, bloodiness, and cruelty,"[8] is left to discover in his present state of loneliness and alienation the fundamental "weakness . . . in all I had built up around me."[9] His isolation is stressed by his frequent refusal to talk to others and his equally frequent irritation with compulsive talkers such as his mother-in-law, Mrs. Almstadt. He has abandoned his reading, has abandoned his writing of biographical essays on, quite ironically, the philosophers of Enlightenment; he all but abandons communication. There is only one subject he talks about, his weariness of life—the life that he observes keenly—and about which he writes copiously. When he creates something, it is an alter ego, but a single alter ego is not sufficient for him. Besides the "I" of the diary, there is the Joseph of a year ago, whose actions and thoughts he describes with mild derision, and there is moreover a voice that he calls Tu As Raison Aussi, a spirit of alternatives. With him he has the two liveliest dialogues of the book.

It would, however, be unfair not to state that Joseph is at least partly justified in his critical attitude toward his former life and his present surroundings. In his first entry he rejects the current "code of the athlete, of the tough boy" that demands a suppression of an inner life and feelings.[10] He is gifted with an acute sensibility that is even heightened by his growing detachment. He is "keenly intent on knowing what is happening to him,"[11] and he realizes, although this is openly indicated only in his dreams, that it may well lead to death. The collective fate he welcomes at the end precludes both an individual future or a sense of hope, as Tu As Raison Aussi clearly demonstrates to him.

Joseph is justified in his fear of an age in which the individual is becoming increasingly less important, he is unfair and subjective only in over-interpreting the signs of this degrading of man. He feels slighted by everybody, by the other tenants, by his sister-in-law, by his niece, by a former party comrade, by a bank manager, and even by the maid who unselfconsciously smokes as she cleans up his room. He takes this as her contemptuous recognition of his unimportance. When his greeting is not acknowledged he screams that he has a right to be spoken to. The bank manager who refuses to cash his check because of his unsatisfactory identification has, of course, a good question when he asks: "How do I know you're this person?"[12] How, indeed, when Joseph hardly recognizes the self he has become under the growing pressure of fear, contempt, and despair.

Joseph, the former idealist, whose talent is for being "a good man"[13] at least asks the right questions: "How should a good man live; what ought he to do?"[14] To profit from the war, to rise socially, economically, or even only as an object of interest in other people's eyes, is contemptible to him: "I would rather be a victim than a beneficiary."[15] What he experiences is the fall from idealism and he indeed becomes a victim, the first in the long row of Bellow's victim-heroes. He suffers from a damaged sense of reality.[16] For this he is partly responsible and realizes that he has no resources that enable him to replace what has been destroyed, but he also, and quite characteristically, refuses to give in completely to the ensuing psychological and philosophical depression. In a typical Bellow-pose he seeks to relate to certain objects that surround him, almost forcefully trying to extract some meaning from them because people have failed to give him the response he needs:

> There could be no doubt that these billboards, streets, tracks, houses, ugly and blind, were related to interior

life. And yet, I told myself, there had to be a doubt.
There were human lives organized around these ways
and houses, and that they, the houses, say, were the
analogue, that what men created they also were,
through some transcendent means, I could not bring
myself to concede. There must be a difference, a quality
that eluded me, somehow, a difference between things
and persons and even between acts and persons. Otherwise the people who lived here were actually a reflection of the things they lived among.[17]

Later, in a passage of great intensity, Joseph
even experiences a certain transformation that
takes place within or through the objects:

The icicles and frost patterns on the window turned
brilliant; the trees, like instruments, opened all their
sounds into the wind, and the bold, icy colors of sky
and snow and clouds burned strongly. A day for a
world without deformity or threat of damage, and my
pleasure in the weather was all the greater because it
held its own beauty and was engaged with nothing but
itself. The light gave an air of innocence to some of the
common objects in the room, liberating them from
ugliness. I lost the aversion I had hitherto felt for the
red oblong of rug at the foot of the bed, the scrap of
tapestry on the radiator seat, the bubbles of paint on
the white lintel, the six knobs on the dresser I had formerly compared to the ugly noses of as many dwarf
brothers. In the middle of the floor, like an accidental
device of serenity, lay a piece of red string.[18]

Yet things remain, or so Joseph hopes, ultimately a reflection of the people who have created
them, and the difficulty in seeing them as such may
be a failing "in us, in me. A weakness of vision."[19]

Joseph realizes that what might save him is the acknowledgment of a common humanity: "goodness is achieved not in a vacuum, but in the company of other men, attended by love."[20] "Humanity," "love," and "grace" are here established for the first time as the central concepts of Bellow's work. The belief in them strengthens Joseph to make an attempt at an acceptance of life, making him prefer embarrassment and pain to indifference, to apathy.[21] Although Tu As Raison Aussi tries to persuade him, he will not become a worshipper of the antilife. He has not done well alone, as he admits at the end before giving himself up to the army. Thus his desire to end his present dangling state by any means whatsoever may be regarded in various ways: as an escape from what he has recognized as destructive, as an attempt to share the fate of his generation, but also as a rash act of giving in to despair and rejecting, for the time being, the responsibility for his own life. As he observes about himself, he may have tried to "strike a balance between what he wants and what he is compelled to do,"[22] but he has not succeeded in achieving the desired equilibrium. No matter which way we regard the final scene, it remains tinged with irony. What Joseph welcomes as a solution bears strong marks of defeat.

With the title of the first novel and its allusions to the pains of indecision and suspension between extremes, Bellow created a powerful metaphor that rivals, among others, Ralph Ellison's

"invisible man" or even T. S. Eliot's "wasteland"
and Malraux's *"condition humaine."* The underlying tradition of the dangling figure is that of the
"underground man," and Bellow's novel draws
indeed on Dostoyevsky's "Notes from the Underground" for its basic situation.

Bellow's earliest published work, the short
story entitled "Two Morning Monologues" (1941),
derives from the same source and anticipates *Dangling Man* in its essential aspects. The "monologue" entitled "Without Work" features another
nameless protagonist invested with unusual sen-
sitivity, whose chief problem is also how to dispose
of time while waiting for induction. Hostility of
the protagonist toward his family, the dreariness
of the urban background, and the atmosphere of
suppressed outrage are all used to stress the necessity of the quest for identity and meaning, which
leads in both stories to a reduction of the self. In
the struggle between alienation and integration
one option can become as meaningless as the other
because identity and self may be lost in both cases.
In all his works of fiction Bellow tries to counter-
balance this dread of annihilation, of the loss of
self, which everybody suffers from, by building the
works around one central character, one distinctly
discernible individual who stands out above the
others by virtue of this very consciousness of himself. The journal form in *Dangling Man* is skil-
fully employed to stress the same point. Although
a prominent fictive "device," it allows for the illu-

sion of an unobstructed view into the heart of the matter as seen from a highly personalized perspective. The need for order and illumination is dramatized by the chaos and darkness that appears during moments of crisis. Bellow's men, though dangling, remain undaunted in their belief in the possibility of the right choice, even if they themselves fail to make it:

> All the striving is for one end. I do not entirely understand this impulse. But it seems to me that its final end is the desire for pure freedom. We are all drawn toward the same craters of the spirit—to know what we are and what we are for, to know our purpose, to seek grace.[23]

Whereas the conflict in *Dangling Man* is internalized in the talks between an "I," Joseph, and Tu As Raison Aussi, in *The Victim,* Bellow's second novel, it is externalized in the relationship between Asa Leventhal and Kirby Allbee. *The Victim* appeared in 1947. This and *Seize the Day* are the most tightly, artfully constructed of Bellow's books. Bellow described in the interview with Gordon Harper[24] that he took great pains with *The Victim,* trying to make it letter-perfect by Flaubertian standards. From the point of view of language, structure, and atmospheric density Bellow succeeded. The style is characterized by great control and restraint. Each new scene contributes to an intensification of the desired effect of oppression. In its wealth of ideas presented and questions raised, the book is a protest against simple solu-

tions. Bellow, as always, is firm in denying his protagonists the easy way out.

Of the two quotations that precede the book,
the first states the theme and the second the mood.
The first, "The Tale of the Trader and the Jinni"
from *Thousand and One Nights,* tells the story of
a traveling merchant who, overcome by heat and
fatigue, rests and eats a handful of dates, the stones
of which he carelessly throws away. The stones
strike the son of an Ifrit and kill him, and the
Ifrit takes his revenge on the merchant. Like the
unlucky merchant, both Leventhal and Allbee are
forced to acknowledge that no action, however in-
significant, is committed in isolation. *The Victim*
is a lesson in the nature of guilt. It is set not in the
merchant's lonely resting place but, to intensify its
meaning, in the city with its myriads of faces that
are described in the second quotation, which is
from *The Confessions of an English Opium Eater.*
Asa Leventhal's New York City, with its teeming
millions, is imbued with the quality of De Quincey's opium dreams.

Leventhal, the editor of a small trade maga-
zine, has a past that is in some stages not unrelated
to Joseph's "dangling." Before he found his present job and relative security he went through a
period of drifting, of being down and out; he then
became a civil servant but gave up his position for
what he thought was a better opportunity. Jobless
again after a few months he turned to friends for
help. Kirby Allbee, a casual acquaintance, sug-

gested Leventhal to his employer, but the exas-
perated, easily infuriated Leventhal lost his temper
during the interview with Allbee's boss. When he
finally found his position as an editor he realized
the value of security and how foolish he had been
to risk it. Instead of being quite comfortably removed from financial worries, as he now is, he
might have become, as he envisions, one of "the
lost, the outcast, the overcome, the effaced, the
ruined."[25] With the emergence of Leventhal's suppressed feeling of shame and remorse the way is
prepared for Allbee's unexpected, Ifrit-like reap-
pearance.

Allbee has chosen a hot summer evening to
seek out Leventhal who does not even remember
his name. On his unsuspecting victim he heaps
accusation upon accusation: Leventhal, by pur-
posely insulting Allbee's former employer during
the interview, has caused Allbee to lose his job and
the love of his wife, who died after she left him.
Allbee holds that Leventhal ruined him in revenge
for an anti-Semitic remark that he, the blond, blue-
eyed Christian of New England descent, had made
in Leventhal's presence. Leventhal, in shock, dis-
may, and contempt, denies even the possibility of
having committed such a petty act and only seeks
to get rid of the seedy, intoxicated Allbee. What
follows is a series of encounters between the two
antagonists, the nightmarish horror of which
verges on the grotesque. Allbee, who never clearly
gives a purpose for his coming except the implicit

one of demonstrating his abject state to the man
he sees as his oppressor, in turn now victimizes
Leventhal by following him, haunting him, encir-
cling him like a quarry. The title of the novel begs
the question, and the answer that is supplied in
the course of the action is that both, indeed all
human beings, are victims. Allbee is in a way a
secularized version of Everyman, and the story,
although certainly no morality play, draws much
of its imagery and symbolism from the theater and
from acting.

The ensuing conflict is as dramatic as it is
grotesque. Leventhal finds that even his best
friends tend to agree that Allbee was possibly fired
because of him and that therefore he is partly responsible for Allbee's present condition. The
original revulsion against an absurd accusation is
followed by the slow emergence of Leventhal's
realization of his guilt and then his acceptance of
it. The more Leventhal allows Allbee to enter his
consciousness, the more he also permits him to
take over his apartment, from which Leventhal's
wife is temporarily absent. Allbee moves in, and
with him come dirt, disorder, and threats in the
dark. Leventhal, however, understands that "this
disorder and upheaval was part of the price he was
obliged to pay for his release."[26] From an attitude
in which he screams at Allbee that he does not
care whether he exists or not[27] Leventhal's outlook
changes to one of recognizing in Allbee the self
that he might have become, had he not "gotten

away with it." Thus Allbee turns into a dark alter ego, a doppelgänger, an exemplification of Leventhal's possible fate.

The identification between the two seemingly unlike characters is achieved with ingenious delicacy: both are paranoic and suspect others of madness. In their minds each creates a terrifying image of the other that has no counterpart in reality; each does so in order to invest the other with his own faults.[28] Each is sure that the other would never be capable of understanding whatever is good and noble in himself, especially not the love each professes to have for his wife.[29] Allbee may be biased against Jews but not any more than Leventhal is biased against Italians. Finally Leventhal even "adopts" Allbee's faults: when he gets drunk it is more an act of identification than of helplessness and despair. The strange attraction that develops between them climaxes in a moment of physical contact in which they touch each other for the first time, not in the spirit of violence but of discovery. It only renews their mutual horror and sets the stage for the final scene. In this Allbee tries to commit suicide in Leventhal's apartment by turning on the gas, but Leventhal, realizing the danger to his own life, throws him down the stairs, hoping to have separated himself from Allbee's suffering forever.

The brief epilogue that takes place several years later contributes another instance to Bellow's ambiguous endings. Leventhal, who now really has a good and secure position, meets Allbee, fittingly, in a theater lobby. Although well-dressed and obviously affluent, Allbee has not lost the underlying look of bad health and decay. He acknowledges his debt to Leventhal, who is at first reluctant even to speak to him. But their business is, and will remain, unfinished. The issues they are dealing with are not capable of a final solution. It is now Leventhal's turn to want to speak to Allbee, who runs away from him and swiftly disappears in the aisles of the theater. Significantly, to indicate the suspended, open state of their relationship, the last phrase that Leventhal tries to address to him is a question.

Any disappointment the reader may feel toward such an unresolved conclusion, however, does not take into consideration the nature of the events described. What we have witnessed is similar in kind to an initiation, a deepening of the understanding; the important thing is not so much the outcome but the process itself. Leventhal recognizes his own increasing awareness of what is going on about him by seeing the elements of his life not as incidents with little connection but as pointers toward a specific meaning:

> Illness, madness, and death were forcing him to confront his fault. He had used every means, and principally indifference and neglect, to avoid acknowledging it and he still did not know what it was. But that was owing to the way he had arranged not to know. He had done a great deal to make things easier

for himself, toning down, softening, looking aside. But the more he tried to subdue whatever it was that he resisted, the more it raged, and the moment was coming when his strength to resist would be at an end.[30]

When Leventhal is first accosted by Allbee, he is a long way from the compassion that moves him in their encounter in the theater. Gradually he learns to face what he has been trying to avoid, the horror, the cruelty, the evil inherent in existence and thus in his own being. Before that, he walks about as if he had his eyes closed; he has "the feeling that he really did not know what went on about him, what strange things, savage things. They hung near him all the time in trembling drops, invisible, usually, or seen from a distance."[31] This distance is shortened by the confrontation with his "victim." The threats that surround him from all sides have to be acknowledged and accepted as part of life.

Leventhal has to overcome his fears of being "blacklisted," of being attacked at night, robbed, and murdered in his sleep, of going insane, not by dismissing the improbability of their realization but by admitting their very possibility and thus his inclusion in mankind. "Human" comes to mean for him "accountable in spite of many weaknesses."[32] He accepts the responsibility for his brother's children during his brother's absence. To save him from neglect, he is ready to take the older boy to live with him. He insists on getting the sick younger child to a hospital although he knows that

the child's mother will blame him for whatever
happens. When the child dies he has to learn to
face her hatred and later even to admit the possibility that this hatred, this enmity, existed only in
his imagination. The "naked malice" he sees in
Allbee's eyes[33] is more likely the gleam of despair.
The sky holds similarly deceptive terrors for him:

> The notion brushed Leventhal's mind that the light
> over them and over the water was akin to the yellow
> revealed in the slit of the eye of a wild animal, say a
> lion, something inhuman that didn't care about any-
> thing human and yet was implanted in every human
> being too, one speck of it, and formed a part of
> him. . . .[34]

Most of all, he has to overcome his own tendency to react to the causes of his fear with violence.
Leventhal is an irascible, easily irritated, violent
person: his wrath turns equally against things,
women, and men. He pushes his wife so that she
falls, he is tempted to jostle his sister-in-law, he
has repeated thoughts of murdering Allbee and
twice comes rather close to doing so. He vehe-
mently pushes against obstructing things like
doors, a symbol of his attempt to escape his claus-
trophobia. He is haunted by the feeling of being
suffocated, by lack of air, by exhaustion. Just as in
the case of Willis Mosby (*Mosby's Memoirs*), remembered guilt literally takes his breath away.
These physical fears are mirrored by the existential
fears he encounters in Allbee's conversation, which
centers heavily on the assumptions that man suf-

fers not only innocently but suffers "for nothing" and that "evil is as real as sunshine."[35] But, Leventhal learns, to be conscious of all this is to be truly alive.[36]

The relation between the single life and the fate of humanity is demonstrated by Leventhal's submergence in the crowds of New York. Leventhal's New York is not simply a city, it is *the* city, the megalopolis of metaphysical dimensions. It harbors De Quincey's sea of faces that rise and fall around Leventhal in mysterious profusion:

> The crowd was extraordinarily thick tonight. . . . He searched for a long time before he found a seat near the pond where a few half-naked children were splashing. The trees were swathed in stifling dust, and the stars were faint and sparse through the pall. The benches formed a dense, double human wheel; the paths were thronged. There was an overwhelming human closeness and thickness, and Leventhal was penetrated by a sense not merely of the crowd in this park but of innumerable millions, crossing, touching, pressing. What was that story he had once read about Hell cracking open on account of the rage of the god of the sea, and all the souls, crammed together, looking out?[37]

Leventhal's trips to his brother's family across the black water to Staten Island evoke further mythological parallels: "The mass of passengers on the open deck was still, like a crowd of souls, each concentrating on its destination."[38] This interweaving of the realistic with the surreal is intensified by the images of heat and oppression. The

introductory paragraph of *The Victim* sets the
tone of exotic strangeness that makes other trans-
formations of the usual into the strange and the
unknown equally plausible:

> On some nights New York is as hot as Bangkok. The
> whole continent seems to have moved from its place
> and slid nearer the equator, the bitter grey Atlantic to
> have become green and tropical, and the people,
> thronging the streets, barbaric fellahin among the stu-
> pendous monuments of their mystery, the lights of
> which, a dazing profusion, climb upward endlessly into
> the heat of the sky.[39]

Although the heat and the presence of the
thronging masses weigh Leventhal down—"he had
the strange feeling that there was not a single part
of him on which the whole world did not press
with full weight, on his body, on his soul"[40]—they
are the necessary catalysts for his fuller realization
of life. They become the terms in which his revelations are expressed. His recognition that "everything, everything without exception, took place as
if within a single soul or person"[41] would be meaningless without the understanding of everyone as
All-bee and of Allbee as everyone. This acceptance
of Allbee—because he is All-bee—is Leventhal's
decisive step toward integration into the society of
man. His realization that "everybody wanted to be
what he was to the limit"[42] becomes the basis for
his newly won concept of brotherhood.

The eye-opening process of Leventhal is accomplished, once more, through dual agents. While

he is in the process of change, things appear to him
"in a new light":

> The walls were flaming coarsely, and each thing—the
> moping bushes, the face of a woman appearing at a
> scream, a heap of melons before a grocery—came to him
> as though raised to a new power and given another
> quality by the air; and the colors, granular and bloody,
> black, green, blue, quivered like gases over the steady
> baselines of shadow.[43]

The brilliant, formerly "unseen" quality of objects
gives him the feeling of being in a foreign city. In
addition he meets people who talk to him in an un-
precedented, significant way, which touches pre-
cisely upon the core of his troubles. The venerable
old Jew Schlossberg raises the very questions that
Leventhal has been trying to answer. Schlossberg
responds to the common plight with an awareness of
death and makes it the basis of his plea for dignity:

> "Here I'm sitting here, and my mind can go around the
> world. Is there any limit to what I can think? But in
> another minute I can be dead, on this spot. There's a
> limit to me. But I have to be myself in full. Which is
> somebody who dies, isn't it? That's what I was from
> the beginning."[44]

The encompassing definition of man as some-
body who still tries to be himself in full, though
death hovers above him, resolves, for whoever
achieves this, the contradiction between man's trying to be more than human and so often ending
up being less than human.[45] A "standard of con-

duct" is needed that will provide guidelines for balance and harmony: "Have dignity, you understand me? Choose dignity"[46] is Schlossberg's counsel. Unable to forego an equivocal piece of philosophy, Bellow lets Schlossberg sum up his advice in an enigmatic phrase that allows various interpretations: "Good acting is what is exactly human."[47] Surface and core, accidental and essential, must melt into each other and become one. It is a measure of Bellow's irony that he leaves it to the individual to decide on the meaning of "good acting." The implied "lesson" is that whatever meaning he finds will be exactly the right one for him.

Dangling Man and *The Victim* are the two novels on which Bellow's reputation as one of the leading exponents of "victim literature" is mainly based. But Bellow is reluctant to talk about these novels and calls the man who wrote them "timid" and "afraid to let himself go."[48] In an interview with Gordon Harper in the *Paris Review* he said that he wrote them with a "borrowed sensibility." Flaubert, James, Camus and even Sartre have been mentioned as possible sources, but the two authors that come immediately to mind for *The Victim* are Dreiser and Dostoyevsky. The resounding quality of the New York background undoubtedly owes much to the Dreiserian city, that place of great accumulations of things, inanimate objects, and of anonymous masses. And the plot seems to have been taken over, complete with incidents, heat, stuffiness, filth, and main characters from Dostoyevsky's "The Eternal Husband." But, when the similarity was brought to Bellow's attention, he could not recall ever having read the Dostoyevsky story, which proves that a "borrowed sensibility" will reinvent the images of hope and horror that suit it.

After the first two novels a released Bellow decided to let himself go. The most significant change in style to date occurred between *The Victim* and his next novel *The Adventures of Augie March* (1953). Of this he said in the interview with Harper: "Why should I force myself to write like an Englishman or a contributor to the New Yorker? I soon saw that it was simply not in me to be a mandarin."[49] From then on, especially in *Augie March* and later in *Herzog,* Bellow was not so much inventing, "constructing" fictive edifices, as listening to what he terms "that primitive commentator." In the same interview he said:

> "When I say the commentator is primitive, I don't mean that he's crude; God knows he's often fastidious. But he won't talk until the situation is right. And if you prepare the ground for him with too many difficulties underfoot, he won't say anything. I must be terribly given to fraud and deceit because sometimes I have great difficulty preparing a suitable ground. This is why I've had so much trouble with my last two novels. I appealed directly to my prompter. The prompter, however, has to find the occasion perfect—that is to say, truthful, and necessary. If there is any superfluity or inner falsehood in the preparations he is aware of it. I have to stop."[50]

With Augie March's story, he never had to stop; the book, he tells us—and we almost forget to take this with a grain of salt—wrote itself. All he had to do was to listen. And what a story it is Bellow catches with his fine ear and unrestrained, released imagination!

2

Bitterness in His Chosen Thing

At the time of the writing of *Augie March* Bellow's output was prolific. In the late 1940s and early 1950s he published several short stories, most of which bear a certain relationship to *Augie March,* and he was also working on two other novels. These, however, he threw away "because they were too sad."[1] One of them was to be called *The Crab and the Butterfly* and contained an episode that Bellow did publish as a short story. This story, "The Trip to Galena" (1950), bears a direct resemblance to *Augie March* both in its conversational tone and in the dilemma of the protagonist, a young man named Weyl.

Weyl, who has been confined to a hospital for several weeks, tells a fellow inmate, Mr. Scampi, about the events on the day when he fell ill. Weyl's sister Fanny, a beautiful girl, was about to marry rich young Neff, who seemed to be socially superior to her. She wanted to introduce her brother as a representative of her family to her future in-laws because she was hoping that he would make a good impression on the Neffs. Weyl was willing to go along with that, but Fanny had another scheme on her mind which he resented. Besides a son, the Neffs had two marriageable daughters and Fanny wanted her brother to marry one of them because, she said, he hadn't done too well by himself.

Weyl has obviously led a varied and economically unsuccessful life; he refers to a time in Europe when he was involved in selling black-market money and goods. Although he had no clear course for his life in mind he refused to let Fanny plan it for him. He tries to explain to Scampi that he is on a kind of quest that he calls his "campaigning":

> "I behaved as if I were campaigning. In the name of what was worth doing, though I never had any idea that what I was doing was worthwhile. . . . You heard me tell my old aunt a while back when she asked me what I wanted, that I didn't want to be sad any more."[2]

Fanny's plotting, her trying to manipulate him and others, evokes in him a deep feeling of revulsion. Her behavior is opposed to his notions of "good conduct in life," which seems to be the main problem occupying his mind: "the next conduct will have to come from the heart, from attachment to life despite the worst it has shown us."[3] The deception he sees taking place on all levels of existence quite literally makes him sick. Unable to put up with Fanny and the Neffs, he rushed off to the train station with a suddenness that Fanny recognized as a sign not of impoliteness but of despair. Nevertheless, as the story ends, we hear that Fanny does not share her brother's insights and is still bent on marrying the young Neff.

The thread that runs through Augie March's story is the theme of the quest for, in Bellow's words, "a worthwhile fate." This quest, this campaign, as one of the minor characters calls it,[4] is Augie's "chosen thing." The bitterness in it for

Augie lies in the fact that he cannot define it. This uncertainty accounts for much of the novel's sadness, which has often been overlooked or disregarded by the critics. It is easy to become absorbed by the exuberance of the novel, by the wealth of incident, character and observation, by the "omnivorousness" of style, to use Ihab Hassan's term. There is no overlooking the new tone in Bellow; he "kicked over the traces, wrote catch-as-catch-can, picaresque."[5] The book is a record of the memories of a man who, in spite of all his questing, remains uncertain of his purpose and essentially lonely. In writing down the story of his life he rarely refers to the time of writing, the present committing of his thoughts to paper, but when he does so it becomes a summary of sadness:

> You do all you can to humanize and familiarize the world, and suddenly it becomes more strange than ever. The living are not what they were, the dead die again and again, and at last for good. I see this now. At that time not.[6]

Augie's efforts are absorbed by a refusal, by saying no to the schemes and plans of others, to the attraction and distraction of things. His strength is taken up by this refusal, which is ultimately a refusal to "lead a disappointed life."[7] And yet, although the book ends with Augie laughing, the prevailing, underlying note is, in Augie's words, that "after much making with sense, it's senselessness that you submit to."[8] Augie's love of the sun does not suffice to dissolve the images of darkness that keep recurring contrapuntally to his quest for light.

Augie, like Bellow, is a Chicagoan; although Bellow was not born in Chicago he grew up and was educated there so that he considers himself a Chicagoan, "out and out."[9] The first sentence of the book sets the mood in more than one way: "I am an American, Chicago born—Chicago, that somber city—and go at things as I have taught myself, freestyle, and will make the record in my own way."[10] The assertion of individuality in these lines is unmistakable. At the same time, it is made clear that the language will be colloquial, and the form of the novel loose. The story, as is usual for the picaresque mode, is made up of a series of episodes that are connected through a central protagonist. Augie's reminiscences, starting from the time when he was about eight, a child in Chicago before the Depression, are carried through the 1930s and 1940s until after the end of the war when we find him in Europe, dealing in black-market goods, married to Stella, the film star, who is on her own somewhere. The novel originally was to be called "Life among the Machiavellians," and it is against these Machiavellians that Augie has to wage his battles.

The first overpowering, dominating figure he encounters is "Grandma" Lausch, the widow of a rich Odessa businessman who has taken it upon herself to live with the Marches, whom she believes unable to subsist otherwise; or, as Augie retrospectively puts it, "she preferred to live with us, because for so many years she was used to direct a house, to command, to govern, to manage, scheme, devise, and intrigue in all her languages."[11] The only person in the family she comes to respect somewhat is Augie's older brother Simon, whom she recognizes as destined for success in this world. Augie's mother, a seamstress, has been abandoned by the father of the children, a laundry-truck driver. For the poor woman in her "love-originated servitude"[12] Grandma has no kind words to spare, but she energetically helps her to manage her life. The only tenderness Grandma ever shows is to Augie's mentally retarded brother, Georgie, and even that is carefully measured out. Augie to her is plainly a fool—unsteady, playful, uncertain of his purpose. Augie admits to all of these, especially to not having Simon's "singleness of purpose."[13] As a result, instead of rising steadily in the world of business he goes from one job to the other: "Saying 'various jobs,' I give out the Rosetta stone, so to speak, to my entire life."[14]

It is always other people who suggest Augie for jobs. At first, Simon tries to take Augie with him on his way up. As boys they both do odd jobs, urged on by Grandma Lausch; Augie distributes theater handbills, then newspapers for his cousin Coblin. Through Simon he is promoted to a news-stand but fails to grasp his first business principle: when he is short-changed by customers he should, according to Simon's ethics, short-change others in turn. But Augie, like Joseph in *Dangling Man,* refuses to profit; since he never ends up with the correct sum he is dismissed. He then gets involved in a petty theft, using most of that money to buy luxurious Christmas presents for his family. When the fraud is discovered, he has to pay all the money back and is punished with the unending contempt of Grandma Lausch. His next employer is the real-estate broker Einhorn.

William Einhorn, a most circumspect businessman and above all a distributor of advice and counsel in all afflictions and crises, even the most uncommon and unforeseen, is a cripple. For him Augie does "unspecified work of a mixed character,"[15] but it is the mixed character that he likes. The work ranges from running errands, helping out with odd jobs, accompanying Einhorn's splendid old father to the beach, to assisting Einhorn in getting dressed, carrying him around on his back, and, most important of all, listening to the story of his life.

Augie, who calls himself "a listener by upbringing,"[16] listens, learns, and sifts the advice. Secretly he rejects as much as he accepts, and it is Einhorn who first recognizes the quality of stubbornness in Augie that derives from his search for a "good-enough fate":

> "All of a sudden I catch on to something about you. You've got *opposition* in you. You don't slide through everything. You just make it look so." This was the first time that anyone had told me anything like the

truth about myself. I felt it powerfully. That, as he
said, I did have opposition in me, and great desire to
offer resistance and to say "No!" which was as clear as
could be, as definite a feeling as a pang of hunger. . . .
I never had accepted determination and I wouldn't
become what other people wanted to make of me.[17]

For telling him the truth about himself, for
giving him so much attention, Augie loves Einhorn
as he will later come to love, if in a different way,
all the other truth-sayers in his life: the bitter but
vivacious Mimi Villars; his great love Thea; Stella,
whom he marries; and his friend Mintouchian,
another, more powerful version of Einhorn. Although his feeling of opposition is as unmistakable
as hunger, Augie is not able to define or explain it.
"I know I longed very much, but I didn't understand for what,"[18] he says, and thus points to a
central feature shared by many of Bellow's characters that is most clearly expressed in Henderson's
repeated and ever incomplete outcry "I want, I
want, I want" (*Henderson the Rain King*).

Meanwhile Augie, after having said no to the
criminal Joe Gorman who wants to involve him
permanently in robbery and fraud, goes to a city
college whose students encompass the variety of the
multicolored city life that appeals to Augie:

. . . the students were children of immigrants from all
parts, coming up from Hell's Kitchen, Little Sicily, the
Black Belt, the mass of Polonia, the Jewish streets of
Humboldt Park, put through the coarse sifters of cur-
riculum, and also bringing wisdom of their own. They
filled the factory-length corridors and giant classrooms

with every human character and germ, to undergo con-
solidation and become, the idea was, American. In the
mixture there was beauty—a good proportion—and
pimple-insolence, and parricide faces, gum-chew innocence, labor fodder and secretarial forces, Danish sta-
bility, Dago inspiration, catarrh-hampered mathemati-
cal genius; there were waxed-eared shovelers' children,
sex-promising businessmen's daughters—an immense
sampling of a tremendous host, the multitudes of holy
writ, begotten by West-moving, factor-shoved parents.
Or me, the by-blow of a travelling man.[19]

In the mixture Augie senses the wealth that
life has to offer to one who chooses wisely and takes
time to consider all options. Augie, for lack of
money, is forced to drop out of college and works
for the Renlings, rich owners of a sporting-goods
store. Mrs. Renling sees that he has possibilities
and wants to change and educate him. She registers
him for evening classes at Northwestern, she
teaches him the ways of the elegant world and asks
him to accompany her to a seaside resort. She even
wants to adopt him, just as Grandma Lausch had
in a way adopted the Marches, as Anna Coblin had
tried to draw him into the family, calling him
"mein kind," just as Tillie Einhorn had treated
him like a son. But, as always, Augie counters
these schemes by his own schemes of evasion. Although he admits that there is something about
him that makes people feel that they want to adopt
him, he has "family enough to suit me and history
to be loyal to."[20] To become like people who are
themselves not at all sure who they are and who

want him mainly to support their own dubious
fabrications of "reality" is not a "good-enough
fate" for him. He prefers to belong to "the world
in general."[21]

Simon, greatly aided by all that he learned
from Grandma Lausch, and by marriage to the
rich Charlotte Magnus, has become wealthy. He
gives in to what Augie has been steadily refusing;
he is "adopted" by the Magnuses and consequently
undergoes the metamorphosis that Augie has
feared and shunned all his life. With all the pressures—those of his own ambition, of his wife and
new family, and of the world of business bearing
down on him—his behavior reaches the stage of
near insanity.[22] Nevertheless he still has an eye on
Augie and tries to do right by his drifting brother.
He arranges for Augie to meet another of the Magnus daughters, Lucy; Augie would not have been
unwelcome as a son-in-law had he thrown himself
into the role Simon is embracing with the same
vigor and conviction as Simon. But when he gets
into a dilemma between old loyalties and his own
profit, he says no again to these splendid opportunities. He prefers to get the sick Mimi Villars to a
hospital and silently take the undeserved blame
of having made her pregnant than to refuse to help
her when she needs him most. Thus he loses the
conventional Lucy.

The financial crash of the Depression has hit
everybody alike. Einhorn is almost a poor man.
Augie sells bathroom paint, unsuccessfully tries to

smuggle immigrants across the Canadian border, works for a service for pampered dogs, takes to book stealing but makes no money because he prefers reading the books to selling them. When he reaches his low as a labor-union leader who is beaten by opponents, Thea Fenchel, a rich and independent acquaintance from the Renling days, seeks him out and takes him with her to Mexico.

Thea, as her name indicates (*thea* is the Greek word for goddess), has something superhuman about her. She calls to mind what Schlossberg in *The Victim* said about the dangers of trying to be more than human. Her enterprises are indeed fantastic. She, too, seeks a worthwhile fate, but what differentiates her from Augie is the conviction that she will find it, not in the "shared condition of all" but in the realms of the exotic. Thus the Mexico where their adventure is consummated foreshadows Henderson's Africa, which is only one of the many parallels between *Augie March* and *Henderson the Rain King*.

The pastoral simplicity, which at first surrounds and enhances their love-making and which deepens Augie's perception of his fate, is, however, revealed as a deception. Nevertheless some of the most moving and stylistically accomplished passages of the novel are devoted to these days in Eden:

> It was afternoon; we were in the Ozark foothills, well off the road, in the woods near a pasture. Up from where we were there was a totter of small pines, and

above them bigger trees, and subsiding land below. Because the water we had was poor we spiked it with rye
for taste. The weather was hot, and the air was glossy,
the clouds white and heavy, rich, dangerous, swagging,
silk. The open ground glared and baked, the wheat
looked like the glass of wheat, the cattle had their feet
in the water. . . . She didn't shut her eyes, but they
were not open in order to see me or anything; filled
and slow, they made no effort but only received and
showed. Very soon I didn't notice either, but knew I
came out of my hidings and confinements, efforts, ends,
observations, and I wanted nothing that was not for
her and felt the same from her. . . .

Meanwhile the clouds, birds, cattle in the water,
things, stayed at their distance, and there was no need
to herd, account for, hold them in the head, but it was
enough to be among them, released on the ground as
they were in their brook or in their air. I meant something like this when I said occasionally I could look
out like a creature.[23]

Through Thea, Augie learns his "creatureliness," the essence of which is a desire for simplicity, here clothed in the metaphor of Arcadian innocence. Creatures play an important role in the
entire Mexican episode. Thea, who catches lizards
and poisonous snakes, attempts to train an American eagle for the purposes of hunting, a dangerous
and near impossible enterprise. The initial stages
of the taming of the eagle, which Augie calls Caligula, represent for him, partly because of the way
Thea imposes her will on the magnificent animal,
the most splendid human act he has ever seen. But
when put to the test by Thea, the eagle fails in the

same way as Augie: Augie takes pity on the lizards, Caligula refuses to kill them.

When Augie is badly kicked on the head by a horse he has fallen off, Thea's response is to sever herself from the losers: she sends Caligula to a zoo and goes off with another man. When this happens Augie "dies somewhat"[24] and never quite becomes his old self again. His old exuberance is quieted by the recognition of certain truths that Thea has made him see: purity of feeling cannot be kept up, complexity will always invade simplicity. Though Thea loved him, she used him for her own purposes. Her parting words are "I have no use for you,"[25] which he counters with a renewed confession of his love. Nevertheless, recognizing that it is impossible to have both love and an independent fate, Augie agrees with Thea's bitter accusation that love would have remained strange to him no matter which way it happened.[26] But this is true mainly insofar as Thea's kind of love is involved, as he later realizes. For her, love is not an end in itself as it is for Augie but an act that sets you free for further action and exploration.[27]

Thea, by the demands she makes on herself, on others, and on life in general, is seeking not only a different kind of humanity but also a different kind of reality; for her, she believes, there must be "something better than what people call reality."[28] People's attempts to construct for themselves this improved "reality" and to recruit others to their version of it[29] are responsible, in Augie's

universe, for most of the existing deception of self
and of one's fellow man. He does, however, learn
from Thea that reality is in the now and here, and
that the only possession is of the moment.[30] This is
the theme that is ironically treated in *Seize the
Day* and also touched upon in *Henderson* and *Herzog*.

After the Mexican episode *Augie March* loses
some of its intensity, which can, of course, be seen
as an indication of Augie's slightly reduced vitality.
In Mexico he rescues the beautiful Stella from the
supposed wrath of a former lover and repeats the
Lucy Magnus–Mimi pattern by doing it in spite of
Thea's pleas. Thea, however, had been deceiving
Augie for a long time. Augie returns to the States
at the time of America's entrance into World
War II. He marries Stella, mainly, one feels, because she says the right words to him. His favorite
project is that of establishing a foster home for
orphaned children somewhere out in the country
where he can unite around him those members of
his family that have been dealt with roughly: his
mother who is living in a home for the blind, and
Georgie who is in an institution. He sees his role
as that of a father, pondering over his unborn children. When Stella tells him that she thinks he will
be a good father, he makes her his wife. It is with
some irony that the more mature narrator says
that a man's character is revealed by what he settles
for and that this, finally, *is* his fate.[31] Stella leaves
him alone a good deal while she is pursuing her
own career as movie star.

On board a troop ship going overseas he becomes the one who gives advice and counsel to
others. Of course he advocates love. After only a
few days at sea, however, the ship is torpedoed and
he barely escapes drowning. His companion in the
lifeboat is another one of those mad schemers and
theoreticians he so frequently encounters, this one
being a scientist. Basteshaw wants to prevent their
being rescued for the sake of his experiments,
which he would be unable to continue should they
be picked up by the enemy. Once more Augie says
no to the course of life that Basteshaw projects for
him; he says no to dying because of Basteshaw's
madness, and uses all his resources to be saved. We
leave him, as the doubtful agent for Mintouchian's
black-market enterprise, alone on the gray coast
near Dunkerque, smiling, even laughing at himself
in his incompleteness, yet still striving to discover
what he cannot define:

> Is the laugh at nature—including eternity—that it
> thinks it can win over us and the power of hope? Nah,
> nah! I think. It never will. But that probably is the
> joke, on one or the other, and laughing is an enigma
> that includes both. Look at me, going everywhere!
> Why, I am a sort of Columbus of those near-at-hand
> and believe you can come to them in this immediate
> *terra incognita* that spreads out in every gaze. I may
> well be a flop at this line of endeavor. Columbus too
> thought he was a flop, probably, when they sent him
> back in chains. Which didn't prove there was no
> America.[32]

In spite of all the contrary advice Augie receives from the "reality constructors"—the later

"reality instructors" of Herzog—he persists in the search for his own fate. Bellow may be giving a clue as to why this desire is so peculiarly powerful when Augie himself denies that it arises from mere obstinacy on his part: "The one thing I could say was that it wasn't merely for my own sake I wanted it."[33] He is obviously trying to prove something that goes beyond the individual life and sees himself somehow as representative of a common plight.

The universality of the theme is expressed by the frequent allusions to historical figures as well as by the quality of richness and abundance, both of things and characters, that pervades *Augie March*. In various essays and stories Bellow touches upon this protean aspect of existence: it may account for life's rich texture, but on the other hand it is the origin of all distractions, the cause of the clear mind's being drowned in a flood of details, perceptions, and temptations. In his essay "Distractions of a Fiction Writer" (1957) Bellow sums up the latter attitude when he complains that today there are

> more things that solicit the attention of the mind than ever before. The libraries and museums are full, great storehouses with their thousands of masterpieces in every style. Their vast wealth excites our ambition. It can make a Dr. Faustus out of many an educated man. It menaces him with death by distraction.[34]

And in the fictive speech called "Address by Gooley MacDowell to the Hasbeens Club of Chi-

cago" (1951) Bellow has Gooley lament along the
same lines:

> "Look at us, deafened, hampered, obstructed, impeded,
> impaired and bowel-glutted with wise counsel and good
> precept, and the more plentiful our ideas the worse our
> headaches. So we ask, will some good creature pull out
> the plug and ease our disgusted hearts a little?"[35]

Augie himself feels overpowered by things,
objects, which have degraded people to the ano-
nymity of being mere users:

> . . . in this modern power of luxury, with its battalions
> of service workers and engineers, it's the things them-
> selves, the products that are distinguished, and the in-
> dividual man isn't nearly equal to their great sum.
> Finally they are what becomes great. . . . No opposing
> greatness is allowed, and the disturbing person is the
> one who won't serve by using or denies by not wishing
> to enjoy.[36]

The last sentence obviously refers to Augie himself and his dread of "too much" of everything,[37]
which Thea also experiences when she refers to
the world as being full of things but empty of people.[38] Augie aptly sums up the view that is expressed in all of Bellow's works when he states that
"in the world of nature you can trust, but in the
world of artifacts you must beware."[39] It is another
example of Bellow's irony when he has Simon give
Augie the advice "not to dissolve in the bewilder-
ment of choices."[40] Simon exemplifies in his own
person just what the other extreme of singlemind-
edness can lead to.

Augie's realization of the dangers of abundance is a relatively late insight; during the greater part of the book he tends to enjoy the wealth of impressions and experiences life has to offer. It is through him that Bellow introduces the copious lists that constitute one of the outstanding stylistic features of the book. By making Augie a sensitive "recording instrument of reality," Bellow succeeds in projecting exquisitely one of his favorite moods: that of the worship of experience, which is, however, not unqualified and not unconditional. As he gives full rein to his love of catalogue he makes Augie a great collector, a *Sammler,* one who is constantly gathering in, not only impressions, often painful ones; not only ideas and world views, often equivocal ones; not only glimpses of the surrounding world and its host of characters; but also words, lists, litanies of words. This verbal exuberance is very much in the tradition of Melville's cetology, of Whitman's triumphantly felt empathy with the totality of the American experience, of Dreiser's urban masses, and of, occasionally, the sharply observant afficionados of the nada, either in the mode of Hemingway or of more recent writers. But Augie succumbs neither to nada nor to "moha," which is explained to Augie as meaning "opposition of the finite,"[41] although often it is from pain that he derives his sense of being alive. When the crazy millionaire Robey, another one of Augie's employers, expresses his longing for a better future for mankind, he does it in terms of enu-

merating man's encumbrances and deficiencies, a
method that Augie heartily endorses. The passage
reads like a melancholy parody of Hamlet's para-
gon-of-animals speech:

> O great age of generous love and time of a new man!
> Not the poor, dark, disfigured creature cramped by his
> falsehood, a liar from the cradle, flogged by poverty,
> smelling bad from cowardice, deeper than a latrine in
> jealousy, dead as a cabbage to feeling, a maggot to
> beauty, a shrimp to duty, spinning the same thread of
> cocoon preoccupation from his mouth. Without tears
> to weep or enough expandable breath to laugh; cruel,
> frigging, parasitic, sneaking, grousing, anxious, and
> sluggardly.[42]

It is, again, the question of the nature of mankind that is being raised. In spite of all the emphasis on man's "creatureliness," which Bellow
stresses by such means as Augie's dreams as well as
by open statements, the final emphasis rests on the
power of man to overcome being merely a creature
and to become a thinking and feeling person.

This is poignantly formulated in another
short fictional work of Bellow's, the "Sermon by
Doctor Pep" (1949). Nobly disregarding the fact
that the "sermon" is being given in "Bughouse
Square, Chicago," Doctor Pep renders Bellow's
views in a splendid piece of rhetoric on mankind,
"being creatures *and* more, having hopes of bril-
liancy, having dread of Acheron . . . embracing
everything with infinite desire."[43] This desire is a
hunger for the real, the actual, even the banal, as

long as it belongs to the total of what man can
experience and be. Augie, in this instance Bellow's
persona, is for the same reason fascinated by great
men, which leads to his almost constant preoccupation with mythological and historical heroes. He
does not hesitate to compare the extraordinary
people he knows to them, thus deepening or rather
qualifying the meaning of personality in mythol-
ogy and history as well as in actual life. Passages
such as the following with their seemingly naive
incongruity account for much of the humor of the
book: ". . . if I were really his [Einhorn's] disciple
and not what I am, I'd ask myself: 'What would
Caesar suffer in this case? What would Machiavelli
advise or Ulysses do? What would Einhorn
think?' "[44] Even when Augie can't sustain the image of himself as "Alcibiades beloved-of-man,"[45]
and when additional historical allusions seem inappropriate, he devotes himself to the more-than-
life-size people—the Coblins with their immense
meals, the towering Magnuses—people who fore-
shadow the figure of the gigantic, crazy millionaire,
Henderson. Like Henderson, Augie embarks on a
pilgrimage into the unknown, whether it be called
Africa or Mexico, on a quest for Man, as he says,
"with a capital M."[46]

It is, however, revealing to observe what happens when Augie does indeed meet an important
historical person. Trotsky is in Mexico at the same
time as Augie; Augie recognizes him as Trotsky
gets out of a car to visit a small-town cathedral.

Augie's reaction seems at first unequivocal: "I always knew my entire life would not go by without my having seen a great man."[47] But when Augie is approached by one of Trotsky's bodyguards, who happens to be an acquaintance of Augie, to render Trotsky an important service, Augie declines: "Please God: I thought, keep me from being sucked into another one of those great currents where I can't be myself."[48]

Augie's preoccupation with great men is revealed as theoretical; he has seen an extraordinary man, and to see is indeed all he wants. The abundance of images of vision in the book is an expression of Augie's desire to see, which is the metaphoric expression of his desire to contemplate. The true vision of things, he says, "is a gift, particularly in times of special disfigurement and world-wide Babylonishness."[49] (Babylonishness is a term Bellow uses to denote the reign of confusion in today's world.) Chicago is Augie's Babel.[50]

These considerations bring up the main objection critics have voiced in regard to Augie's character: Augie is passive, things happen to him, he does not cause things to happen. To this, one feels tempted to say: Well, who does? But there are more appropriate explanations for Augie's behavior. It is true that it is always another who suggests a course of life for him, who plans, and schemes. Augie sees these projections for what they are: various possible roles that he tries on the way one tries on clothes.[51] Ironically, all the main "schemers" in his life—Mrs. Renling, Thea, Simon —do indeed buy Augie elaborate wardrobes of beautiful clothes. He willingly puts them on and willingly casts them off. They are symbols of his consideration of possibilities and ultimately of his refusal to play any "role" at all. It has been mentioned that Augie's strength is committed partly to this refusal. But most of it goes into another struggle, equally nonpositive and almost absurd— the struggle to avoid the violence that he regards as the hallmark of his age. Or, to phrase it more affirmatively, he struggles to uphold those qualities that he recognizes as most human: tenderness and dignity. He does not take Simon's advice to cheat the honest customers; he does not take Einhorn's advice to triumph over Simon at an opportune moment; he flatly rejects Einhorn's precept that

> "one should make strength from disadvantages and make progress by having enemies, being wrathful or terrible; should hammer on the state of being a brother, not be oppressed by it; should have the strength of voice to make other voices fall silent—the same principle for persons as for peoples, parties, states."[52]

The only "scheme" Augie ever nurses is the foster home for orphans, and through it he plans to redeem the violence that has been done to his idiot brother, to his mother, to innocent children.

Augie's helpfulness has not been adequately recognized by critics. He is ever ready to assume responsibilities, to keep promises that others should have kept. He never refuses his help to his friends whatever the risks and the losses he will incur. In the scenes in which he assists Mimi in getting into a hospital and Stella in escaping from her jealous lover he displays a strength of character and an unbreakable will that make any suggestion of passivity seem inappropriate. Granted that, he has his faults and is a "fool," a schlemiel, in minor matters. Yet the important decisions he makes are those of an admirable human being. Gooley MacDowell in his address sums up my interpretation of Augie as well as the state of the times when he says that today "even to be decent needs heroism."[53]

There is another side to Augie's supposed lack of action. He believes in revelation, the kind of revelation that arises from emptying one's mind of the superfluous, the distracting, in order to concentrate on the essential. These revelations may come as a state of being rather than a mental recognition, and they may be elicited by the shape of objects that suddenly assume a rare beauty. This recalls a favorite device of Bellow in the earlier novels:

> I drank coffee and looked out into the brilliant first morning of the year. There was a Greek church in the next street of which the onion dome stood in the snow —polished and purified blue, cross and crown together, the united powers of earth and heaven, snow in all the clefts, a snow like the sand of sugar. I passed over the church too and rested only on the great profound blue. The days have not changed, though the times have. The sailors who first saw America, that sweet sight,

where the belly of the ocean had brought them, didn't
see more beautiful color than this.[54]

A similar example stresses the function not
only of the actual experience but also of the memory of it, and thus places Bellow in the line of development that runs from Proust to Nabokov:

> And often that is how the trees, water, roads, grasses
> may come back in their green, white, blue, steepness,
> spots, wrinkles, veins, or smell, so that I can fix my
> memory down to an ant in the folds of a bark or fat in
> a piece of meat or colored thread on a collar of a
> blouse. Or such discriminations as where, on a bush of
> roses, you see variations in heats that make your breast
> and bowel draw at various places from your trying to
> correspond; when even the rose of rot and wrong
> makes you attempt to answer and want to stir.[55]

The most important passage in connection
with Augie's deepening understanding of life and
himself is his description of what he calls the "axial
lines" of life:

> "I have a feeling," I said, "about the axial lines of life,
> with respect to which you must be straight or else your
> existence is merely clownery, hiding tragedy. I must
> have had a feeling since I was a kid about these axial
> lines which made me want to have my existence on
> them, and so I have said 'no' like a stubborn fellow to
> all my persuaders, just on the obstinacy of my memory
> of these lines, never entirely clear. But lately I have
> felt these thrilling lines again. When striving stops,
> there they are as a gift. I was lying on the couch here
> before and they suddenly went quivering right straight
> through me. Truth, love, peace, bounty, usefulness,
> harmony! And all noise and grates, distortion, chatter,

distraction, effort, superfluity, passed off like something unreal. And I believe that any man at any time can come back to these axial lines, even if an unfortunate bastard, if he will be quiet and wait it out."[56]

Augie emphasizes again and again that truth comes as a gift when striving stops, when one commits oneself not to becoming but to being, as Henderson will describe it. This accounts for the pleasure Augie takes in retiring to places where he can be undisturbed, gratefully taking in the rays of the sun, whether it is on board ship, in a garden in Mexico, or in a courthouse square:

> A state that lets you rest in your own specific gravity, and where you are not a subject matter but sit in your own nature, tasting original tastes as good as the first man, and are outside of the busy human temper, let free even of your own habits.[57]

It is important to keep in mind that Augie's desire for life in the sun is not motivated by a shunning of action or a rejection of consciousness but arises from his knowledge of darkness, the darkness which he says has widened his outlook.[58] The passages that deal with this darkness are the most powerful and the most original in *Augie March*. In them Bellow has achieved stylistic perfection. The harmony of tone and mood is the mark of his unmistakable voice:

> Now there's a dark Westminster of a time when a multitude of objects cannot be clear; they're too dense and there's an island rain, North Sea lightlessness, the vein of the Thames. That darkness in which resolu-

tions have to be made—it isn't merely local; it's the
same darkness that exists in the fiercest clearnesses of
torrid Messina. And what about the coldness of the
rain? That doesn't deheat foolishness in its residence of
the human face, nor take away deception nor change
defects, but this rain is an emblem of the shared condition of all. It maybe means that what is needed to
mitigate the foolishness or dissolve the deception is always superabundantly about and insistently offered to
us—a black offer in Charing Cross; a grey in Place
Pereires where you see so many kinds and varieties of
beings go to and fro in the liquid and fog; a brown
in the straight unity of Wabash Avenue. With the
dark, the solvent is in this way offered until the time
when one thing is determined and the offers, mercies,
and opportunities are finished.[59]

The seventeenth-century grandeur of this
rhythm seems to come straight out of John Donne's
sermons. It is this same darkness that Augie faces
at the desolate beach near Dunkerque, aware, once
more, of the loss of Eden, of the vanished "liquid
noon" (Bellow's phrase for the classical age) of the
Greeks, and of the triumph of violence. In this ob-
scuring darkness it takes all of a man's courage
even to believe in the existence of human beings.
But this belief, as Bellow has pointed out elsewhere, suffices for the time being.[60]

A look at the first two novels seems to indicate
that Bellow had to pass through a "literary" phase
before he could turn to the resources of actual
experience. *Dangling Man* and *The Victim* demonstrate that he was not free from a modern di-

lemma, that of having to see life in terms of literature, of the preexperienced, preformulated,
second-hand, once-removed. Mailer deplores this
state of things, Thomas Pynchon ridicules it, William Burroughs and Rudolph Wurlitzer are driven
to a denial of the imagination to rid themselves of
it. With *Augie March*, Bellow left the borrowed
forms and sensibilities and embarked on a literary
quest of his own. Himself one of the *"vrais voya-
geurs"* alluded to in *Augie March*, he wrote the
book "in odd corners of Paris, and, afterwards, in
Austria, Italy, Long Island and New Jersey."[61] By
introducing the motif of the journey and the term
picaresque in the interview with Harvey Breit,
Bellow did place the book into another, older literary tradition. Although it is hard to see Augie as
downright rogue, Lazarillo de Tormes, Simplicius
Simplicissimus, the novels of Fielding, Smollett,
and Sterne do come to mind. Huck Finn and Hol-
den Caulfield in *The Catcher in the Rye* have
also been mentioned as literary relatives of Augie's, because of their youth, their naiveté, and
their unrestrained manner of talking about themselves. *Augie March* has even repeatedly been
called a *Bildungsroman*. If we have to resort to
the German at all, I would suggest the more correct label of *Entwicklungsroman* because the emphasis in *Augie March* is decidedly not on Augie's
encounter with objects of culture as it is in
Goethe's *Wilhelm Meister*, the prototype of the
Bildungsroman. No course in Western civilization

or life-time reading plan could satiate Augie's desire for experience. Nevertheless, the measure of
his growth remains questionable as well. Augie is,
more than an advocate of "Bildung" and self-
development, a champion of reality. This also
serves to explain what it is that makes him write
down his memories. The motivation lies in his relation to the world, in his longing for reality:
"Reality comes from giving an account of your-
self."[62]

3

The Dread
Is Great,
The Soul
Is Small

Especially when seen in the light of *Mr. Sammler's Planet,* Bellow's most recent novel, *Seize the Day,* which appeared in 1956, seems indicative of a basic struggle for formal and stylistic control in which Bellow was engaged from the beginning of his career as a fiction writer. The nine years that elapsed between *Augie March* and *Seize the Day* also point toward Bellow's attempt to come to terms with two diverging aspects of his talent: emotional intensity arising from shared suffering on the one hand, and the awareness of the necessity of artistic control on the other. This explains at least partly the fluctuation between the open and closed forms of Bellow's novels and his vacillating between tight and loose modes of language. Whereas *Dangling Man* and *The Victim* belong to the "restrained" category, *Augie March* belongs in the other category.

"In *Augie March,*" says Bellow, "I discovered rhetoric but I didn't have it under control. I decided that I would let it be experimental. This would be my revolt against classical form."[1]

At the time of the writing of *Seize the Day,* Bellow was preoccupied with the subject of order and harmony, especially the order that fiction imposes on reality, and with the transformation of the concept of order into fictive shapes. He ar-

---

rived at a conclusion that declared his independence as a writer:

> In a work of art the imagination is the sole source of order. There are critics who assume that you must begin with order if you are to end with it. Not so. A novelist begins with disorder and disharmony, and he goes toward order by an unknown process of imagination. And anyway, the order he achieves is not the order that ideas have.[2]

It is interesting to note the stress Bellow places on the "unknown process" and the distinction he makes between the kind of order being imposed by the imagination and the kind of order ideas have. Bellow, who has repeatedly been called the intellectual among living American novelists and who occasionally finds it necessary to defend the right of the novelist to think—but never for the sake of ideas alone[3]—persists in giving precedence to the structures of the imagination over those of the intellect. The reason for this may be seen in his belief that if a reconciliation between man's godlike state and his wretchedness can be achieved, it will be through an imaginative vision of the *"condition humaine"*:

> The dread is great, the soul is small; man might be godlike but he is wretched; the heart should be open but it is sealed by fear. If man wretched by nature is represented, what we have here is only accurate reporting. But if it is man in the image of God, man a little lower than the angels who is impotent, the case is not the same. And it is the second assumption, the subangelic one, that writers generally make. . . . On

> the nobler assumption he should have at least sufficient
> power to overcome ignominy and to complete his own
> life. His suffering, feebleness, servitude then have a
> meaning. This is what writers have taken to be the
> justification of power. It should reveal the greatness of
> man. And if no other power will do this, the power of
> the imagination will take the task upon itself.[4]

With *Seize the Day,* Bellow returned to what
he calls the "delights of discipline,"[5] which demands of him constant revision of his writing. The
conflict between the loose and the tight forms also
expresses itself in the changing narrative perspective in Bellow's novels: four of the seven longer
works of fiction that have appeared so far are written from the first-person point of view; the three
others from that of a narrator who talks about the
protagonists in the third person. In this, as in various other aspects, *Seize the Day* resembles *The
Victim* more closely than either *Dangling Man* or
Augie March, which are both written in the first-
person form. It seems of some significance that the
last published novel again reverts to the third person. In *Mr. Sammler's Planet* Bellow has come
more closely than in his other works to achieving
the balance between a truly human, i.e. a "partici-
pating" outlook on life, and the simultaneous realization of imaginative order.

Seize the Day, then, contains elements that
are familiar from former works. The protagonist,
forty-four-year-old ex-Hollywood actor, ex-sales-
man Tommy Wilhelm, is another victim. When

the story begins he is mainly a victim of his own
wrong decisions. He gave up college to become an
actor; after seven years of stubborn work as an
extra he returned to the East, got a job as a sales-
man but left the company when an outsider received the promotion he had been promised. He
also broke up his marriage because, for reasons he
cannot clearly state, he feels unable to continue
to live with his wife. Now he has to support her
and the two children although he has no job. He is
living in the Ansonia Hotel on the upper West
Side, where his father Dr. Adler, a highly respected
retired physician, also resides. In his desperate
situation Tommy seeks his father's help, but Dr.
Adler, who arrogantly and coldly has no compassion for victims, refuses to give it. Tommy turns to
a Dr. Tamkin, who leads a shady existence as psy-
chologist, healer, and hawker of great ideas. He
promises Tommy salvation, financial as well as
otherwise, and for this purpose introduces him to
his philosophy of *carpe diem* and to the art of
speculating in the commodities market. Tommy
hands his last seven hundred dollars over to him,
whereupon Tamkin disappears. Tommy, who
tries to trace him in the crowded streets of New
York, is carried forward by the pushing masses into
a funeral parlor, where he finally breaks down,
weeping for himself, the dead stranger, and the
state of the world.

Just as for Augie, things for Tommy have
been too complex, and he longs for simplicity; but

unlike Augie, Tommy makes more and worse mistakes than he can bear. He not only falls acci-
dentally into the hands of Tamkin—who as another Machiavellian and fast-working theoretician,
is the fascinating descendant of the protagonist of
one of Bellow's earliest works, "The Mexican General"[6]—but knowingly gives himself up to this man
whose falseness he perceives. He is attracted by
"the peculiar flavor of fatality in Dr. Tamkin,"[7]
so that after having known him he will have known
the worst that could ever happen to him. Possibly
he is attracted even more by Tamkin's articulate-
ness. Tamkin's power of speech, his great persua-
siveness, contrasts sharply with Tommy's lack of
verbal facility; it is even hinted that a slight speech
impediment caused his failure as an actor. From
Tamkin, who constantly juggles words like "eternal," "elemental," "the real universe," "nature,"
"anxiety," "spiritual compensation," etc., he hopes
to get what he cannot achieve himself: a definition
of his fate. Tommy, then, is more than somewhat
masochistic, childish, and given to self-deception.
He is another erector of ideal constructions, a
would-be believer in false hopes, given to specula-
tion in both senses of the term. But he takes all his
wrong steps out of a deep inner need that is greater
than he can bear.

    The New York environment is used to mir-
ror, enhance, and partly explain his confusion.
Just as for Asa Leventhal, the city becomes his
pressure chamber in which he dies imaginary

deaths of suffocation and drowning. The thronging crowds of *The Victim* have lost nothing of their dread:

> And the great, great crowd, the inexhaustible current of millions of every race and kind pouring out, pressing round, of every age, of every genius, possessors of every human secret, antique and future, in every face the refinement of one particular motive or essence—*I labor, I spend, I strive, I design, I love, I cling, I uphold, I give way, I envy, I long, I scorn, I die, I hide, I want.* Faster, much faster than any man could make the tally. The sidewalks were wider than any causeway; the street itself was immense, and it quaked and gleamed and it seemed to Wilhelm to throb at the last limit of endurance.[8]

New York is Babel, and since obsession with himself is written on everyone's face, communication has become impossible. Everybody speaks his own language, has his own private system of thinking. Tommy greatly suffers from the lack of a common idiom even for the simplest thoughts: "You had to translate and translate, explain and explain, back and forth, and it was the punishment of hell itself not to understand or be understood."[9] The choice the individual faces is only that of a more or less violent and not always merely metaphoric death. The Ansonia Hotel with its clientele of the aging and decrepit, the Broadway neighborhood in the West Seventies and Eighties, which is populated by so many older people, are the fictional instruments of preparation for the final scene in the funeral parlor.

Much has been made of the images of drowning in *Seize the Day*. The hotel elevator that carries Tommy seems to sink endlessly downward; objects appear as if reflected in water; Tommy dreads visiting the underground baths and massage rooms of the hotel; he uses an electric razor so as to avoid contact with water; and he is finally indeed "drowned" in his flood of tears. With obvious irony on the narrator's part Tamkin urges Tommy on toward this "death by water": "To know how it feels to be a seaweed you have to get in the water."[10] Equally ironically Tamkin boasts of having invented an underwater suit in which one could supposedly walk for miles on the bottom of a river. Tommy is doomed in any case for trusting in Tamkin's "inventions." The images of suffocation serve the same purpose. They are superseded in importance only by the images of weight. Life is the burden under which Tommy breaks down:

> The spirit, the peculiar burden of his existence lay upon him like an accretion, a load, a hump. In any moment of quiet, when sheer fatigue prevented him from struggling, he was apt to feel this mysterious weight, this growth or collection of nameless things which it was the business of his life to carry about. That must be what a man was for. This large, odd, excited, fleshy, blond abrupt personality named Wilhelm, or Tommy, was here, present, in the present . . . this Wilky, or Tommy Wilhelm . . . was assigned to be the carrier of a load which was his own self, his characteristic self. There was no figure or estimate for the value of this load. But it is probably exaggerated by the sub-

ject, T. W. Who is a visionary sort of animal. Who has
to believe that he can know why he exists.[11]

The "business of life" as a metaphor is taken
from the central death symbol of the novella,
which is money. The place of the killing is the
stock market where people go "with murder in
their hearts":[12]

Money-making is aggression. That's the whole thing.
The functionalistic explanation is the only one. People
come to the market to kill. . . . Only they haven't got
the genuine courage to kill, and they erect a symbol of
it. The money. They make a killing by a fantasy.[13]

Surprisingly, it is Tamkin who teaches
Tommy these truths. But Tamkin's rare truths are
exactly the cause of the fascination that is exerted
on Tommy as well as the reader by Tamkin, who
has the insights of a fallen angel. For every hundred falsehoods, Tommy comes to understand,
there is at last one truth.[14] Although Tamkin is a
con man, his philosophy contains ideas of value.
He succeeds in explaining to Tommy's satisfaction
where the confusion about himself is coming from.
He maintains that it arises out of the clash between
the "pretender soul," the server of the "society
mechanism" that destroys individuality, and the
suppressed "real soul," out of which arise Tommy's
true and ultimate needs. The various names that
Tommy has been given or has adopted represent
unconscious efforts to establish an identity: "In
Tommy he saw the pretender. And even Wilky

might not be himself. Might the name of his true
soul be the one by which his old grandfather had
called him—Velvel?"[15] Tommy Wilhelm is the
name under which he had hoped to have a Holly-
wood career; he had rejected Wilhelm Adler, the
name his father had given him, thereby incurring
his father's anger and later contempt. And in rejecting Velvel he denied his Jewishness. The three
names are plainly reminiscent of Joseph's three
personae in *Dangling Man.* Tamkin recognizes
Tommy's particular relationship to each name and
ingeniously addresses him with the name that will
touch the quick at that moment and thus best
serve his dark purposes.[16] This is one of the ways in
which he makes Tommy docile, ready for his
philosophy of "seize the day," which teaches the
prime importance of the present moment: "Bringing people into the here-and-now. The real universe. That's the present moment. The past is no
good to us. The future is full of anxiety. Only the
present is real—the here-and-now. Seize the day."[17]
And in the very act of demonstrating the validity
of this truth, Tamkin deceives Tommy: while he
urges him to seize the here-and-now and to help a
blind, old man across the street, he escapes with
Tommy's money. Thus Tamkin's philosophy is
acted out at the expense of Tommy's financial collapse.

The ending of the story is wholly in the tradition of ambiguous Bellow endings. We do not
know why Tommy is crying. But Tamkin, the

"confuser of the imagination,"[18] has nevertheless brought about release and relief, even if by fraudulent means. There is another, nobler side to Tommy than would seem to be hidden in this large, sloppy caricature of a body: Tommy is capable of genuine emotion and of a self-transcending love. With this love he loved his mother who is now dead. He loves his children, and is a father in a truer sense than Dr. Adler. He even experiences a moment of loving unity with those crowds that formerly made his soul shrink:

> And in the dark tunnel, in the haste, heat, and darkness which disfigure and make freaks and fragments of nose and eyes and teeth, all of a sudden, unsought, a general love for all these imperfect and lurid-looking people burst out in Wilhelm's breast. He loved them. One and all, he passionately loved them. They were his brothers and sisters. He was imperfect and disfigured himself, but what difference did that make if he was united with them by this blaze of love?[19]

It is a longing for this love that enables him to experience visions of the true "business of life":

> . . . he received a suggestion from some remote element in his thoughts that the business of life, the real business—to carry his peculiar burden, to feel shame and impotence, to taste these quelled tears—the only important business, the highest business was being done.[20]

Tommy, crying at the bier of a stranger, affirms suffering, gives himself up to it as to the supreme moment, and thus derives through the experience of pain a sense of his existence. His affirmation of suffering may be understood as an affirmation of humanity, as a recognition and acknowledgement of what he shares with other human beings. Bellow has again stated one of his basic themes.

The peculiar relationship that Bellow's characters have to objects is also apparent in *Seize the Day,* though in an ambiguous way. On the one hand, objects seem to defy Tommy, who likens himself to a "loose object" aimlessly sliding around in a "tilted" America.[21] The newspaper pages slide away from him, cigars go out before he expects them to, his hat, as he puts it, refuses to "defend" him.[22] On the other hand, objects fulfill the same revelatory function as in the earlier novels. Waterglasses cast "small hoops of brilliance"[23] on a white tablecloth and make Tommy conscious of the sunshine, for which he feels a need similar to the need Augie feels. The fact that this image recurs as an introduction to Tommy's reminiscence of the blaze of love he feels for the people on the subway makes it the symbol of Tommy's fantasy of a better, more truthful, more loving world:

> There sons and fathers are themselves, and a glass of water is only an ornament; it makes a hoop of brightness on the cloth; it is an angel's mouth. There truth for everybody may be found, and confusion is only— only temporary, thought Wilhelm.[24]

The unities of time and place are effectively observed in *Seize the Day.* A similar tightness and neatness of construction characterizes most of Bellow's short stories. *Seize the Day* was published in a volume that also contained three short stories ("A Father-to-be," "Looking for Mr. Green," "The Gonzaga Manuscripts") and a one-act play, *The Wrecker*. Tony Tanner has aptly pointed out in his monograph on Bellow[25] that one of the connecting links between these five works is the motif of money, especially money as a symbol of corruption and "Babylonishness." The attitude toward money is a measure of the characters' worth. In "The Gonzaga Manuscripts," which immediately calls to mind James's "Aspern Papers," a young American travels to Spain in search of the lost manuscripts of his favorite Spanish poet. He hopes to trace them through the former mistress of the poet. His experiences in Spain are an uninterrupted series of confusions, deceptions, and misunderstandings. The precious manuscripts, as he finally gets to know, were buried with the woman. Spanish society ridicules him, the police repeatedly search him, and, in the place of the poems, he is offered shares in a pitchblend mine in Morocco, which, the Spaniards are convinced, will fulfill every American's "ultimate need" as they promise financial prosperity.

To a great extent money causes the problems in the lives of the protagonists of the other two stories. In "Looking for Mr. Green" a welfare check is to be delivered to a Negro by that name. But George Grebe, whose job it is to deliver it, cannot find Green in the maze of the Chicago slums. Much as he is convinced that it must be possible to match person and name, the real and its symbol, he only succeeds in deceiving himself into believing that Mr. Green can be found.

Rogin, the father-to-be, is another one of Bellow's heroes who has visions on the subway. While on his way to his beautiful yet extravagant fiancée who squanders his money, Rogin sees a middle-aged man on a subway car who could be the son he and Joan might one day have. He looks like them both, combining the negative qualities of his parents without their redeeming merits. Rogin nearly cries with pity at the sight of this "ordinary, clean, rosy, uninteresting, self-satisfied, fundamentally bourgeois face."[26] He resolves to be stricter with Joan, not to indulge her any more in her wasteful ways. Yet she senses his mood and drowns his criticism in a sensually rich scene in the bathroom, where she washes his hair with fragrant shampoo and streams of "green, hot, radiant water."[27] Ideas, precepts, logical conclusions do not, Bellow seems to be saying, shape our lives. "A Father-to-be" provides in Joan the first glimpses of Herzog's beautiful, domineering wife Madeleine, and of Herzog's strange moments of relief and recovery in the sensual surroundings of the bathroom.

The Wrecker, the one-act play, presents an individual caught in the dilemma of either accepting money and being ruled by the forces that offer it as bribe, or remaining himself and doing things his own way. The character called "husband" would prefer destroying the condemned building in which he has been living for the past years and forgoing the city's compensation money to being jostled and pushed around by the "society mechanism." His defiance climaxes in his wrecking and tearing apart his own apartment.

Houses and apartments frequently assume a symbolic quality, especially in the later Bellow. The apartment in *The Wrecker* symbolizes to some extent the man's not altogether successful marriage, the family life that has taken place within its walls. It is the wife's comic insight that "maybe the best way to preserve the marriage is to destroy the home."[28] This is followed by a thunderous crash.

A similar crash also terminates *A Wen* (1965), another of Bellow's one-act plays (most of which are unpublished). The scientist Dr. Ithimar gazes with equal absorption at electronic particles and tiny wens. When lightning strikes his hotel, the end of the world for Ithimar seems to have come together with the end of his visual ecstasies. As in *The Wrecker,* the "grotesque dimensions" of ordinary life are made visible by means of the dramatic action as well as by the fantastic yet perceptive statements of the characters. Ithimar utters one of Bellow's central tenets when he says that "the human mind is a slave of its own metaphors,"[29] a theme that the later Bellow repeatedly takes up in his fiction as well as his critical essays.

The early short stories, such as "The Mexican
General," "Two Morning Monologues," "The
Trip to Galena," often have the quality of serving
as try-out pieces for longer works. Bellow's more
mature stories, especially those published in his
most recent collection *Mosby's Memoirs* (1968),
are more finished, polished, and complete in themselves. Besides reprinting the three stories from
Seize the Day, Mosby's Memoirs contains "Leaving
the Yellow House," "The Old System," and "Mosby's Memoirs." The last two are of particular interest because they are the first fiction that Bellow
published after his best work to date, *Herzog*
(1964).

Especially in these three stories, the realm of
the mind emerges as the "setting," the place of
enactment of whatever is happening to the protagonists. The lonely old woman in "Leaving the Yellow House" reconsiders the events of her life as
she is trying to formulate her last will. Mosby, of
course, does the same, as he writes his memoirs.
And in the most interesting of the three, "The
Old System," the retired scientist Dr. Samuel
Brown spends the better part of a short winter day
in bed, reminiscing, musing, reexperiencing his
love for the figures of his past. This Dr. S.B. (note
the initials) can claim kinship with Herzog, whose
book also takes place almost entirely in the mind.
The fact that in all three instances the experiencing consciousness is that of someone old foreshadows Mr. Sammler. It is a distinct indication of a

new turn toward the sublimity of the loving-yet-detached attitude that Bellow has developed within the last five or six years.

Bellow's mastery of a modified interior monologue, which he makes heavy use of in most of his works, is generally acknowledged. He develops it into a highly versatile vehicle for a twofold purpose. One is to illustrate the character's imprisonment within himself, a restrictiveness that separates him from others. The other is to illuminate the turmoil of mental activity that continuously overwhelms the characters, frequently changing their concept of reality. Therein lies the danger of these ever-germinating, freely sprouting ideas: that they make the imagined seem more real and sometimes more worthwhile than the actual. Needless to say, they sometimes do provide a self-generated gratification and comfort as well. Sometimes, however, the basic idea can be so frightful that it keeps haunting the mind, spreading silent dread and involving the better part of the characters' energy in the struggle against it. In *Seize the Day*, in the stories in *Mosby's Memoirs* as well as in *Henderson the Rain King* (1959), and certainly in *Herzog*, it is the fear of death, the insuperable task of having to come to terms with it, that provides the ultimate link between these works.

4

Every Guy Has His Own Africa

*H*enderson the Rain King (1959) is a book by a man who wishes to believe in the triumph of the imagination. Whatever remains unresolved about it may possibly be explained by the fact that Bellow wishes so intensely, imagines so intensely, yet realizes incompletely. Much is stated but not demonstrated; much is left unsaid, possibly on purpose, possibly because it proved literally unimaginable. *Henderson*, the book with the most quixotic hero, is Bellow's most poetical novel. A middle-aged American millionaire, cast-off son, war hero, and breeder of pigs, he listens to inner voices, experiences ecstasies in nature, performs rituals, and talks anything but business talk. Who but Bellow would allow such a person with such contradictory features to say that a woman smiles "as steady as the moonlight at the bottom of a stream"[1] or that an African tribe stricken with drought has "to feed on the bread of tears"[2]—and still have him remain not only credible but moving?

The best approach to *Henderson*, which has been called a fable and a romance, is the one suggested by Bellow himself in another context. Speaking in general about books whose content is heavily symbolic, Bellow says: "The beauty of the book cannot escape you, if you are any sort of reader, and it is better to approach it from the side of naiveté than from that of culture-idolatry, sophistication and snobbery."[3] The Africa in which Henderson has his adventures is not the Africa of the geography books nor Hemingway's Africa nor the Africa of anthropologists, although it features magnificent landscapes, hazardous hunting scenes and an assortment of rituals and reenacted myths. It is, however, related to Conrad's dark continent. It is a "remote place," which someone has been sent to colonize, as Bellow points out in an essay called "Some Notes on Recent American Fiction."[4] There Bellow also mentions an "Alaska of the soul," "a barren emptiness" within the colonist himself that has to be brought under cultivation.[5] It is no coincidence that besides Africa, the land of the Eskimos and wintery Newfoundland play decisive roles in the novel. Alaskas and Africas of the soul have much in common: every "guy" who suffers from the waste of his life has his own Alaska and his own Africa, which by means of extreme cold and extreme heat, by utter lack of life and by an intensification of all life forces, confront him with the essential, the elemental, the irreducible.

Among Bellow's work, *Henderson* is most closely related to *Augie March*. Although the motif of the search for a new mode of conduct in life is touched upon in the previous books and is explicitly treated in old Schlossberg's plea for dignity and mobility, it is not elevated to a central theme until *Augie March*. In *Augie March,* Bellow initiated formulations that prefigure the formulation of Henderson's basic dilemma. At the end of *Augie March,*

Augie sums up the underlying motivation for his adventures: "I have always tried to become what I am.
But it's a frightening thing."[6] Henderson's craving
to turn from a Becomer into a Be-er is here anticipated by the terror it evokes in the individual who is
faced with the necessity of having to answer, in fear-
ful isolation, the ultimate philosophical question.
Like Augie, Henderson is on a quest and knows it.
There is in both books the exotic setting. Henderson, like Augie, has a particularly intense relationship with animals. His longing, like Augie's brother
Simon's, results in violent action, and it is this violence that Henderson has to overcome. It is indicative of his struggle against the basic dread of all
Bellow's heroes: the fear of annihilation. Henderson is, to quote Doris Lessing's phrase, one of the
"children of violence." He sees and experiences
life in terms of violence. He is impatient, intoler-
ant, and even brutal; existence, as he says, has become odious to him.[7] By his violence he partly expresses his impotent anger at a life that he can
neither bear nor change. This is the reason for his
sudden trip to Africa. Like Faulkner's Ike McCas-
lin ("The Bear"), like Mailer's D.J. (*Why Are We
in Vietnam?*), he accepts the idea of relinquishment,
deciding that on the road to salvation one must
leave everything behind.

So at a rather advanced age he leaves for Africa to hunt for the healing here and now. His
faithful black guide Romilayu first takes him to the
remote tribe of the Arnewi, a friendly people,

whose chief, Itelo, has been educated in Beirut. Henderson is welcome, although the land of the Arnewi has been stricken by what is expressly referred to as a curse, which is a drought during which most of the cattle of the tribe have died. A large reservoir of water is still full, but it is taboo because other creatures have chosen to live in it: thousands of frogs bar the Arnewi from using the precious water. Henderson immediately takes up the cause and puts his ingenuity at the disposal of Itelo and his people. Though strangely reluctant to accept his offer, they do not prevent him from carrying out his plans. While Henderson seemingly imbibes the wise words and precepts of old Queen Willatale, who teaches him "grun tu molani"—i.e., man wants to live, all creatures want to live—he, unaware of the contradiction, plots the destruction of the frogs. He lusts "to let fall the ultimate violence on these creatures in the cistern."[8] Thus he is led by his temper to behave not only like a clown but like a fool or worse in the eyes of the Arnewi. He very cleverly constructs a bomb that he plants in the cistern, with some risk to his own life. He does succeed in killing the frogs. The explosion, however, is so violent that the retaining walls are also destroyed and all the water is lost. Henderson departs in shame from the silent Arnewi.

Romilayu, timid and faithful like Sancho Panza, then takes Henderson to the land of a tribe so remote that decades have passed since the arrival

of the last stranger. Nevertheless the Wariri capture and treat the two visitors like enemies, subju-
gating them to various trials and tests of endurance
before Henderson is allowed to see their ruler.
Strangely enough, King Dahfu is not only a well-
educated man who almost graduated from medical
school but a philosopher of some depth who is familiar with William James and the psychoanalyst
Wilhelm Reich. The rough treatment of the
travelers was partly because of internal tensions between him and his court. He and Henderson soon
develop mutual admiration, understanding, and
friendship. Dahfu not only knows the answers to
Henderson's questions, he also lives by them.
"King, I am a Becomer," Henderson says to him.
"You are a Be-er."[9] Dahfu recognizes Henderson
as an "avoider" who cannot live with the knowledge of his inevitable death. He therefore develops a plan to make Henderson face the inevitable
and transcend his fears.

Henderson has to prove himself worthy of
such friendship. Taking part in a highly stylized
ceremony to induce rain, he performs an extraordinary feat of physical strength by lifting the
idol Mummah. When the miraculous takes place
and rain starts to pour down from a formerly
cloudless sky, he is elevated to the position of
Sungo, or rain king. His rank is equal to that of the
king since he may, under certain circumstances, become his successor.

Dahfu then acquaints Henderson with the

source of his unusual spirituality and serenity. Under his palace, in a dark den, he keeps the lioness Atti, whom he has tamed. Dahfu is convinced that he has absorbed lion qualities from the lion that will enable him to perform the stupendous task his tribe is expecting of him. The Wariri believe that at the death of a king his soul enters a lion cub, which his son, who has now succeeded him as king, has to capture and tame. At his first attempt, Dahfu captured the "wrong" lion, Atti, but kept her against the opposition of a superstitious court.

Henderson is to meet Atti, because, so Dahfu believes, she can teach him to overcome his anxiety. She will, in Dahfu's phrase, remove the "ego emphasis" through her beauty and will cause "consciousness to shine."[10] Because she is "all lion," "one hundred per cent within the given,"[11] she will demonstrate to a trembling Henderson what it means to be what one is to the limit.

Dahfu wants Henderson to come to terms with the basic issue; in a scene of magnificent intensity Henderson faces the lion, faces death, transcends his fear, and, through imitating the animal's sound and motion, "is" the beast.[12] Dahfu is exhilarated at having put his theories to a successful test. When the day comes to hunt again for the lion his father inhabits, he honors Henderson by taking him along, thus inviting him to share his fate. Henderson accepts although he senses tragedy. The lion that is captured castrates and kills Dahfu. Henderson, his official successor, is held captive by the apprehensive tribe but manages to escape together with Romilayu and another lion cub, which, according to the belief of the Wariri, now contains Dahfu's soul. He boards a plane back to the States with the intention of finally realizing his long-suppressed desire: under the name of Leo E. Henderson he will enter medical school.

Henderson maintains that "something of the highest importance" has been revealed to him that he is obliged to communicate;[13] the book thus takes the shape of a report addressed to "you people,"[14] which is Bellow's clever device for writing in the mode that is his forte. Throughout his work we hear this energetic talking voice that demands and commands attention.[15] In this *Henderson* resembles Ralph Ellison's *Invisible Man,* whose protagonist also perceives the rendering of his account as a social act. This idea of service that culminates in Henderson's final choice of profession pervades the book, and the changes it undergoes are indicative of Henderson's development. Henderson, like Joseph, madly throws himself into World War II —an act whose purpose is to deaden his sensibilities and quiet his inner voice. He then decides to produce food. Out of defiance, to spite his wife, his neighbors, and the rest of the world, to show the world that it is a pig,[16] as he puts it, he establishes a pig kingdom on his inherited "cursed" land. It is then that his inner voice declares its want with the greatest urgency. When he reaches the Arnewi he insists on putting his technical ingenuity at their disposal, with disastrous results. Western technology not only cannot save but also drains the life-giving substances, if applied without wisdom. By lifting Mummah and thus producing rain for the Wariri, he has for the first time accomplished his desire—to effect a useful deed. He has, however, done so without realizing that this may bring about his own death. No service to a community is truly valid without identification with this community.

This is, in essence, what Dahfu has to teach him. Dahfu attempts to demonstrate it through identification with the lion, whom he believes to be a superior creature. Henderson who thinks of himself in terms of animals—pigs, cats, frogs, lions, bears, etc. represent to him certain states of mind and decisive steps in his life—is inherently inclined to accept Dahfu's theories concerning Atti. But in the moment preceding Dahfu's death Henderson realizes the fallibility of Dahfu's ideas: the theory of the possible conversion of the soul may be right but the object chosen to demonstrate it, the wild beast, is wrong. To his prayer for the doomed king, "the thought added itself that this was all mankind needed, to be conditioned into the image of a ferocious animal."[17] It is Dahfu's tragic nobility that actually teaches the lesson, his life, not his ideas. By returning from civilization into the wilderness of his tribe, by willingly submitting himself to possible death in the framework and context of his culture, by living joyfully "in the knowledge of annihilation" and by avoiding all easy escapes, Dahfu bears witness to the possibility of a more brilliant reality and thus becomes the agent of Henderson's redemption.

Henderson has repeatedly been called a comic hero, and Bellow himself labels the book a satire.[18] The various myths that are used enforce, at least partly, the impression of parody: Henderson as "God" who lights a thornbush in the desert, Henderson as Sir Percival who takes the curse off a wasteland, Henderson as the exemplary hero of redemption-resurrection myths, Henderson as young Hercules at the parting of the ways, Henderson as Daniel in the lion's den. Yet the urgency of his outcry for salvation—"What shall I do?"[19] he cries, using the words Christian speaks when he reaches ultimate despair (in *Pilgrim's Progress*)— calls forth certain doubts about the level of such parody. Two other aspects of the book stress the serious concern underlying the comic surface: the nature of the revelations through objects and colors that Henderson shares with most of Bellow's other protagonists, and the conjuring powers attributed to the imagination, a subject that no author of Bellow's standing would take lightly.

To counteract all accusation of "improbability," Bellow has introduced the possibility of seeing the whole book as the rendering of a dream. Henderson repeatedly states that he feels like a dreamer; furthermore, there are references to his madness and a fever from which he suffers throughout his "trip." The more appealing interpretation lies in regarding Henderson's adventures as adventures in the mind, adventures created by a powerful imagination:

> And believe me, the world is a mind. Travel is mental travel. I had always suspected this. What we call reality is nothing but pedantry. . . . The world of facts is real, all right, and not to be altered. The physical is all there, and it belongs to science. But then there is the noumenal department, and there we create and create and create.[20]

This attitude makes it easier for the skeptics to accept the states of ecstatic communion with objects that Henderson experiences, objects from which he receives orders[21] and with which he feels a unity that can only be described as mystical:

> It is very early in life, and I am out in the grass. The sun flames and swells; the heat it emits is its love, too. I have this self-same vividness in my heart. There are dandelions. I try to gather up this green. I put my love-swollen cheek to the yellow of the dandelions. I try to enter into the green.[22]

Henderson converts himself into "the green." Thus he follows Dahfu's basic tenet that "what homo sapiens imagines, he may slowly convert himself to."[23] In this creative conversion through the imagination Dahfu sees hope for a truly noble man: "Think of what there could be instead by different imaginations. What gay, brilliant types, what merriment types, what beauties and goodness, what sweet cheeks or noble demeanors. Ah, ah, ah, what could be!"[24] In Henderson, Dahfu found the companion soul to share his ecstatic belief in the powers of the mind: "Imagination, imagination, imagination! It converts to actual. It sustains, it alters, it redeems!"[25]

What is conviction for Dahfu remains, at least for some time, an unreality to Henderson that has the character of a fervent wish:

> What? Well, for instance, that chaos doesn't run the whole show. That this is not a sick and hasty ride, helpless, through a dream into oblivion. No, sir! It can be arrested by a thing or two. By art, for instance. The speed is checked, the time redivided. Measure! The great thought. Mystery! The voices of angels![26]

This desire that it be so is, of course, Bellow's very own. Henderson he has designated as the character most like himself, "the absurd seeker of high qualities."[27] It is this identification that makes it improbable that *Henderson* is primarily a satire. The signs of actual change in Henderson are the imaginative product neither of a self-distanced mocker of mankind nor of an unrealistic enthusiast but rather of a melancholy former participant who remains an undaunted adorer of life.

This lack of actual change has been criticized as the major flaw of the book. But this is to misunderstand Bellow's intention, which is suggested repeatedly through the work. First, one might question whether the successful realization of a character in a contemporary novel should be judged primarily by the "change" he undergoes. Rebirth

happens only in myths. Henderson does not so
much change as *intensify* what he is, thus illustrat-
ing the meaning of the transition from Becomer to
Be-er. "Intensify rather what you are. This is the
one and only ticket,"[28] he is told by one of his revelatory voices. Second, Bellow has the habit of sub-
merging his characters in significant experiences
that bring them up to a critical point at which
change might occur, without actually showing the
forms it is going to take. His novels conclude "with
the first step. The first *real* step."[29] There is, then,
the firm belief in the possibility of a new start in
life. But faced with the fact that every "guy" is at
least as incommensurable as his Africa, Bellow declines the posture of omniscient author, choosing
humility before judgment.

5

---

*History,
Memory–
That Is What
Makes Us
Human*

*H*erzog is not just a novel but an education.[1] It comprises, as has often been stated, the whole of the Bellow cosmos: the characters, incidents, ideas, stylistic idiosyncrasies, the seemingly casual form, the intense authorial presence, the Jewishness, the humor, the city background, of the former books are all reassembled here to reflect an original, erudite, elegant and restless mind. *Herzog*—thus far—contains the final synthesis of what Bellow has learned as a writer. He himself states that in writing this novel he was completing a development, "coming to the end of a literary sensibility. This sensibility implies a certain attitude toward civilization—anomaly, estrangement, the outsider, the collapse of humanism."[2] The scope of the book is indicated by these terms. *Herzog* is no less than a fervent defiance of pessimism concerning the human condition in the present time. *Herzog* is an education, a representative book, in another sense: to anyone not familiar with the quality of life in the United States during the 1960s the study of *Herzog* will provide a most rewarding and amazingly comprehensive introduction. Middle-aged Professor Moses Elkanah Herzog, although an intellectual, a big-city Jew—and probably quite mad—is, nevertheless, a representative man and American.

Of course the book has strong autobiographi-

Excerpts from *Herzog* reprinted by permission of The Viking Press, Inc. Copyright © 1961, 1963, 1964 by Saul Bellow.

Excerpts from *The Last Analysis* reprinted by permission of The Viking Press, Inc. Copyright © 1962, 1965 by Saul Bellow.

cal traits, as Bellow readily admits. Asked about the sources of the book, he said that "every writer borrows what he needs from himself."[3] The resemblance between some aspects of Herzog's experience and those of Bellow is undeniable, as the childhood episodes in Canada demonstrate. Herzog uses the same words to describe his "ancient times. Remoter than Egypt"[4] that Bellow uses in describing his childhood:

> I was born into a medieval ghetto in French Canada. My childhood was in ancient times which was true of all orthodox Jews. Every child was immersed in the old testament as soon as he could understand anything, so that you began life by knowing Genesis in Hebrew by heart at the age of four. You never got to distinguish between that and the outer world. Later on, there were translations: I grew up with four languages, English, Hebrew, Yiddish and French. . . . It was a verbal environment."[5]

Herzog's mother, whose mind is "filled with old legends, with angels and demons,"[6] very likely resembles, at least in the descriptions, Bellow's mother, "a figure from the Middle Ages."[7] Occasionally it is possible in this context to observe Bellow at work: little pieces of "reality," remarks that have remained in Bellow's consciousness and are reported elsewhere as "facts," reappear in *Herzog*. One example is the comment of a student—who is tactfully kept anonymous—that "art is for Jews."[8] An even more characteristic example—because the hurt seems to have been deeper—is the opinion

offered to Bellow when he was a college student:
Jews, whose cultural era has long since passed, will
never be able to understand a civilization based on
Anglo-Saxon Protestant values, will never be able
—especially not as sons of Russian immigrants—to
get the right feeling for English words.[9] A passage
repeating the same bias appears in another essay as
well and is taken over almost verbatim into *Herzog*.[10] Henderson, the only Christian hero in Bellow's fiction, starts his "pig kingdom" to spite a
Jew. In what is perhaps a similar assertion of spite,
Moses Herzog becomes a professor of history, and
Bellow, the son of Russian Jewish immigrants,
turns into a writer.

    Herzog is a realistic novel, *Herzog* is a psycho-
logical novel, *Herzog* is a novel of ideas, *Herzog* is
partly an epistolary novel. Thus it seems contrary to
Henderson. But Henderson's fervent wish to believe
in the power of the imagination finds its equivalent
in Herzog's craving to believe "that reason can make
steady progress from disorder to harmony and that
the conquest of chaos need not be begun anew every
day. How I wish it! How I wish it were so! How
Moses prayed for this!"[11] The conquest of chaos may
be taken in both cases, Henderson's as well as Herzog's, to refer ironically to the protagonists' private
lives, for one thing. Herzog's is in a state of not-alto-
gether-undeserved confusion. Mainly because he was
bored, he had divorced his first wife Daisy, who now
takes care of their son, Marco, and had given up a
comfortable, orderly, and respectable existence as

university professor and scholar of some promise. After a series of love affairs he married Madeleine Pontritter, the beautiful, extravagant, brilliantly intelligent daughter of a once famous impresario. Madeleine wanted him to concentrate wholly on his scholarly work, so Herzog bought an enormous, old, dilapidated house in Ludeyville in the Berkshires, which it became his job and pastime to fix. At that time Madeleine betrayed him with his best friend, Valentine Gersbach. The Herzogs, including their little daughter June, and the Gersbachs then moved to Chicago because Madeleine could not bear to be buried in a village away from intellectual life. The hitherto unsuspecting Herzog was told about her unfaithfulness. Although he still loved her, Madeleine divorced him.

Herzog was greatly shaken by the failure of his second marriage and by the twofold betrayal of wife and friend. He realized, however, that it was a quid pro quo: what he had done to Daisy, Madeleine was inflicting on him. He knew that he deserved what he suffered.[12] The unhappiness, frustration, anger and despair remained nevertheless, so much so that he began to lose his bearings and even contemplated revenge on the adulterous pair. What he diagnosed as possibly incipient insanity drove him to a series of rash trips from New York to Martha's Vineyard, back to New York, from there to Chicago and then to Ludeyville, all within a few days.

The bulk of the novel is taken up by Herzog's

recollection of the days of these trips. In the Berkshires, lying in a hammock in his wild garden, Herzog relives and reexperiences his former life. Thus
the actual "present" of the novel occupies only two
pages at the beginning and a few more at the end,
while everything else takes place in Herzog's singu-
larly active mind. The sentence at the very beginning that sets Herzog thinking—"If I'm out of my
mind, it's all right with me"[13]—is repeated shortly
before the end, when Herzog emerges from his
thoughts, thus indicating the borderlines between
"action" and reflection.

The narrative perspective is complicated by
the fact that Herzog not only remembers but remembers himself remembering, not only thinks
but thinks about himself thinking, and it is the
content of these secondary memories and reflected-
upon ideas that is of utmost importance for an
understanding of Herzog's character and predica-
ment. The protagonists of these memories of memories, instead of appearing twice removed and suit-
ably remote, take on the overpowering appearance
of being more alive, more imbued with reality,
more vividly present than the people with whom
Herzog has actual contact, like his brother Will or
his friend Ramona. The figures of his childhood
and youth in Montreal and Chicago—his parents,
friends, and relatives—loom larger than any other
figures in the book. It seems plain that the stature
of these people and the diminishing importance of
all others indicate Herzog's love for them, reveal
the richness of emotion they continue to elicit from

him: "Whom did I ever love as I loved them?"[14] Thus he creates his world in his mind.

Herzog is a novel of ideas, of thought-processes, in the wide sense of the term. Herzog is preoccupied not only with personal memories and continual reflections on those memories. In addition, as a professor of history he has appropriated the doubts, the knowledge, the suggestions and the wisdom of the last four centuries and relates them all to himself, to his own strivings and problems. As Bellow says, he "tests them first upon his own sense of life and against his own desperate need for clarity. With him, these thoughts are not a game. Though he may laugh as he thinks them, his survival depends upon them."[15] He sees himself in a historical context and is therefore overwhelmed by both the importance of his role as a responsible philosopher and by the burden of correcting the fallacies and misconceptions he encounters.

Retrospectively, but only so, his own "role" takes on a comic aspect: "The progress of civilization, indeed, the survival of civilization—depended on the success of Moses E. Herzog. And in treating him as she did, Madeleine injured a great project."[16] The first step toward the improvement of the human condition seems to be the preservation of himself—this is the reason Herzog now recognizes as underlying his frantic taking of sleeping pills. He was endeavoring to get sleep enough to clear the mind he so valued so that he could continue to think.

Herzog is not only a prisoner of perception,[17]

as he calls himself, and a prisoner of memory, he is
also the captive of his own tendency toward compulsive thinking as he re-analyzes the basic questions of Western philosophy. His dissertation on
*The State of Nature in 17th and 18th Century
English and French Political Philosophy* led him
toward an intense study of the concept of Romanticism, which in turn became the basis for his
highly regarded book *Romanticism and Christi-
anity.* He was trying to complete a second volume
during his retreat to Ludeyville, but he abandoned
the project, feeling that it was absurd to profess to
have all the answers in his field of study while being unable to overcome the confusion of his private
life.

It is next to impossible to indicate briefly the
wealth of ideas touched upon in the novel, or, for
that matter, the number of famous personalities
adduced, attacked, questioned, and frequently re-
futed—Rousseau, Condorcet, Proudhon, Spinoza,
de Tocqueville, Spengler, Nietzsche, Heidegger, to
mention only a few, as well as contemporaries and
colleagues of Herzog. The main line of thought,
however, to which Herzog returns over and over
again, has to do with the misconceptions introduced by Romanticism into Western thinking, especially in its popularized form:

> I intended in the country to write another chapter in
> the history of Romanticism as the form taken by ple-
> beian envy and ambition in modern Europe. Emergent
> plebeian classes fought for food, power, sexual privi-

leges, of course. But they fought also to inherit the aristocratic dignity of the old regimes, which in the modern age might have claimed the right to speak of decline.[18]

This right to speak of decline, of giving in to despair too easily and as a matter of fashion, is denied by Professor Herzog. He attacks, sometimes with flaming seriousness, sometimes with biting irony, what he calls a cheap, unjustified pessimism:

> The canned sauerkraut of Spengler's "Prussian Socialism," the commonplaces of the Wasteland outlook, the cheap mental stimulants of Alienation, the cant and rant of pipsqueaks about Inauthenticity and Forlornness. I can't accept this foolish dreariness. We are talking about the whole life of mankind. The subject is too great, too deep for such weakness, cowardice—too deep, too great. . . .[19]

Herzog cannot and will not agree that the West is doomed, as he was taught as a student. The "inspired condition," he believes, is not the prerogative of a few—a conception based on an exaggerated Romantic notion of the self. Nor does he see it as having been obliterated by a mass civilization:

> . . . to live in an inspired condition, to know truth, to be free, to love another, to consummate existence, to abide with death in clarity of consciousness—without which, racing and conniving to evade death, the spirit holds its breath and hopes to be immortal because it does not live—is no longer a rarefied project. . . . Annihilation is no longer a metaphor. Good and evil are real. The inspired condition therefore no visionary

matter. It is not reserved for gods, kings, poets, priests, shrines, but belongs to mankind and to all of existence.[20]

What is necessary for man is a new attitude toward "reality" that is less hostile and is founded on the belief of the compatibility of this reality with the "law of the heart."[21] Herzog's uncompleted study was to have shown "how life could be lived by renewing universal connections,"[22] a valid concern for a man suffering from lack of understanding and loneliness.

The improvement of human life, Herzog recognizes, can occur only with change, a change of heart that will induce a change of life. The "miracle of his altered heart,"[23] which Herzog experiences, could not have been effected without some concept of its hoped-for results, but even that may not be enough for mankind:

. . . the problem as I see it is not one of definition but of the total reconsideration of human qualities. Or perhaps even the discovery of qualities. I am certain that there are human qualities still to be discovered.[24]

Herzog starts on this complete reassessment of values by ascertaining, through the confrontation and struggle with past and present representatives of various doctrines, first, what human life is *not*. Man's life is *not* a business;[25] it is *not* a continual crisis preceding ultimate corruption;[26] it is *not* a meaningless prelude to certain death,[27] although death has to be accepted on its own terms. It is not even a thinking-process,[28] a notion that Herzog has difficulty in parting with. Thought, he finally concludes, may simply turn into a further realm of confusion, if man is given to "the delusion of total explanations."[29]

The "dream of man's heart," a phrase strongly reminiscent of "his heart's ultimate need" in *Seize the Day*, is "that life may complete itself in significant pattern."[30] Herzog's use of the term pattern means a disavowal of self-centeredness and a turning toward meaningful relationships: "The real and essential question is one of our employment by other human beings and their employment by us."[31] Herzog, when he finally reaches these conclusions, and with them arrives at the end of his compulsive thinking for the time being, feels a deep longing simply to share with other human beings and an overpowering eagerness to *begin*.[32] His change is indicated by his reconciliation with the painful necessity of repeated "fresh starts" in life.[33]

It is again interesting to note how closely these reflections of Herzog resemble the ideas propagated by Bellow in his critical essays and reviews. As early as 1956 Bellow took a positive stand against philosophical pessimism,[34] and in the following years, especially during the time of the writing of *Herzog*, he rarely passed up an opportunity to deride the false Cassandras of the Western world. The very formulations anticipate *Herzog*. In Bellow's essay "The Writer as Moralist" we recognize and doubly relish, after reading *Herzog*, such phrases as "despairing sauerkraut, a side dish to the knackwurst of middle-class Promethianism"[35] or, in a short piece entitled "A Comment on 'Form and Despair,' "[36] diatribes against the doom of the West as being "the Established Church in modern Literature."

The style of *Herzog* is also clearly anticipated in an important essay on "The Future of Fiction." The function of great fiction, even if it concerns itself with such topics as hate and despair, will always be "to create scale, to order experience, to give value, to make perspective and to carry us toward sources of life, toward life-giving things."[37] The same essay expresses again the familiar concern with the nature of human beings, a topic that is also explicitly dealt with in Bellow's comments on "Fiction of the Fifties": "We cannot make the final assessment of human value. What we are inclined to do, however, is to renew the inquiry, abandoning old historic and aesthetic conceptions."[38]

"Where Do We Go from Here: The Future of Fiction" also contains one of the basic tenets of Bellow's code as a writer: "The imagination is looking for new ways to express virtue."[39]

Herzog's "virtue" has been very much at the center of the critical discussion of the book. Any *Bildungsroman*—and *Herzog* is a *Bildungsroman* in the true sense of the term—must, by definition, deal extensively in ideas, using them both as a yardstick to measure the character's maturity and as a stepping-stone toward that maturity. Yet critics have suggested that Herzog fails to come to terms with ideas: that he is either drowned in them, thus evading action or commitment (a comment resembling the criticism of *Augie March*), or that he ignores them, following instead those emotional impulses that lead him and the novel toward an easy, unconvincing resolution.[40] That no "resolution" is intended, beyond the simple taking of the "first step," has already been mentioned.

It seems that the function of ideas in *Herzog*, and the state or condition to which they lead the protagonist, has not been well understood. Ideas in *Herzog*, like memories, primarily serve as a basis to establish a standard of "conduct" in the intellectual realm, as a corrective for one's views, as something against which to measure one's own interpretations. They occasionally serve as a source of emotional relief in that their expression brings release. What is most important, however, is Herzog's changing attitude toward ideas in the various stages of his development. Again, as with memories, the change is effected through the later confrontation with what Herzog once believed, "experienced," thought. Reminiscing for Herzog means a reliving of his former life to find a new attitude toward the past, to himself, and therefore inevitably to the present. When he remembers his selfishness and callousness toward his mother, he now experiences the full measure of shame and guilt that he formerly had evaded. He "reaches" the present a wiser man, having at the same time—through his renewed and intensified suffering—atoned for his old guilt.

Rethinking ideas that have been basic to his studies over the years, Herzog also arrives at new conceptions. Much of what used to burden him is revealed in its irrelevancy, is disclosed to him as a great mass of nonsense, as "distraction" (in Bellow's special sense of the term) that has to be rejected if one wants to survive: "We have to dismiss a great number of thoughts if we are to have any creaturely or human life at all."[41] "Private life," plagued by such ideas, can become humiliating, shameful, and paralyzing. What is erroneously considered the privilege of intellectuals may turn out to be merely "another form of bondage."[42]

Thus Herzog's growing maturity, his "change" is indicated not by his acting—or not acting—according to ideas but by his discarding them. The subtle, muted humor of the book arises mainly from Herzog's description of his former selves, his mild comments on what he calls the "earlier avatar of his life,"[43] his various roles as victim, lover, avenger, scholar, saver of mankind. He watches himself going through the motions of being all of these and rejecting each of them, outgrowing them one by one. He could, for instance, have become "Moses, the old Jew-man of Ludeyville, with a white beard, cutting the grass under the washline with my antique reel-mower. Eating woodchucks."[44]

The woodchucks, of course, give him away as not being entirely serious about his former "projections" of such careers.

It is also true that, although he suffers deeply, he thinks of himself as comical "to the point of death."[45] "Personalities," Herzog says, "are good only for comic relief."[46] He sees himself, his wife, and her lover as "a comedy team . . . with me playing straight man."[47] If married to his friend Ramona, their union might easily yield material for a "vaudeville show."[48] His secret wish of many years—that in dealing with fate, it might be possible to exchange goodness and willingness for "preferential treatment"[49]—has led him to constantly "being on a meek kick."[50] Again, the phrase betrays his altered attitude toward himself.

Herzog's own tone makes it impossible to consider *Herzog* another item of victim literature. Bellow himself, intending the novel as a break away from it,[51] consciously turned toward comedy. *Herzog*, in his words, "makes comic use of complaint."[52] Herzog, who says about himself that he "hates the victim bit"[53] and comes to see suffering as "another bad habit"[54] or simply a waste of time, is able to put his victim persona behind him exactly because he discards his old notions of himself and of "personality" in general. He may have been a victim, often of his own destructive tendencies, but he is now a "survivor," as all people living in this present age are survivors.[55] What the novel

shows is the lifting off of a heavy burden, a great
pressure, that leaves the protagonist in a state of
relief, not to say redemption.

This point about Herzog's final state of being
—Herzog's own realization, at least in certain moments, of an "inspired condition"—brings us to the
critics' second target of attack, namely the inac-
tivity and the easy resolution of the hero. As the
misunderstanding of the novel as victim literature
clearly demonstrates, it was by no means easy for
Herzog to achieve the peace of mind with which the
novel concludes. Lying in his hammock, absorbing
the sun and the clear, fragrant summer air, gathering flowers, cooking simple meals may seem un-
worthy activities for a man of Herzog's intellectual
potential. But for someone who has possibly
warded off insanity, they represent an achieve-
ment. At the end Herzog has succeeded in chasing
away the dark shadows of the past; he has freed
himself of misconceptions, of a burdensome "personality," of wasted emotions, and especially of
feeling love for a woman who has ridiculed and
rejected him. He has reached an equilibrium in
which the absence of desires is balanced by an absence of pain.

Herzog is, to quote one of Bellow's most
deeply felt and brilliantly worded metaphors in
the novel, a man "whose breast feels like a cage
from which all dark birds have flown—he is free,
he is light."[56] He is ready for a new experiencing
of life with its "unexpected intrusions of beauty."[57]

In an image of great significance for the resolution of the book Bellow describes the way in which Herzog is overcome by a feeling of near gratitude and affirmative acceptance, of "being well satisfied to be, to be just as it is willed, and for as long as I may remain in occupancy."[58]

> He loved to think about the power of the sun, about light, about the ocean. The purity of the air moved him. There was no stain in the water, where schools of minnows swam. Herzog sighed as he said to himself, "Praise God—praise God." His breathing had become freer. His heart was greatly stirred by the open horizon; the deep colors; the faint iodine pungency of the Atlantic rising from weeds and mollusks; the white, fine, heavy sand; but principally by the green transparency as he looked down to the stony bottom webbed with golden lines. Never still. If his soul could cast a reflection so brilliant, and so intensely sweet, he might beg God to make such use of him.[59]

This taking-in of beauty and the resulting state of mind exemplify the presence and working of "inspiration," "grace," a redemptive power, or whatever one wants to call it, in the novel. This passage, as well as some others, could be cited to clear up the misunderstandings concerning the hierarchy of values in Bellow's fictional world. Bellow himself leaves no doubt about his intentions: "I think a good deal of *Herzog* can be explained simply by the implicit assumption that existence, quite apart from any of our judgments, has value, that existence is worth-ful."[60] Passages such as the above reveal the "spontaneous, mysterious proof" that

Bellow requires for the justification of life, a proof "that has no need to argue with despair."[61]

Besides the desire for a fresh start in life and the belief in a meaningful existence, Herzog has another feature that is common to many of Bellow's protagonists: his extreme intensity, in which he greatly resembles Henderson. Herzog gives himself wholly to whatever he thinks, feels and experiences. He "becomes" part of his surroundings, of the cities and even the houses he inhabits;[62] and they, in turn, become the symbols of his ambitions and assumptions, like his grand "estate" in Ludeyville. With people, historic or contemporary, he identifies to a degree that enables him to have insights even into characters totally uncongenial or hostile to himself, so that in his running mental commentary he produces brilliantly sharp descriptions of the host of lawyers, doctors, childhood figures, colleagues, psychiatrists and so forth that he has encountered on his "vague pilgrimage."[63] Most of all he identifies with the sufferers, the innocent victims of gratuitous evil that remains an inexplicable phenomenon for him. His intense compassion is one of Herzog's most redeeming features, ennobling a character that he himself designates as narcissistic, masochistic, and anachronistic.[64]

The intensity of Herzog's experiencing convinces him that there is a meaning inherent in this intensity. Even if he cannot delineate its nature by words, he is willing to accept this very intensity itself as meaning:

And this is the unwritten history of man, his unseen, negative accomplishment, his power to do without gratification for himself provided there is something great, something into which his being, and all beings, can go. He does not need meaning as long as such intensity has scope. Because then it is self-evident; it *is* meaning.[65]

Herzog, like Henderson, craves use, craves "employment" by other human beings. But after several false starts he realizes that his most painful mistakes originated from his vain attempts either to "save" people, as he tried to save Madeleine, or to be "saved" himself by them. Therefore he will not, in spite of his strong temptation to give in to the same pattern one more time, agree to marry the enticing Ramona, or to hand himself over to a hospital, or to accept substantial financial support from his two rich brothers. He refuses to accept any more advice, especially not from the Reality Instructors who use "facts" as punishment. He refuses to enact any more histrionics, to play any more roles. The aim of his undirected intensity, he hopes, will be to divest his versions of the real of their artificiality, to divest the world of himself[66] so that meaning may shine through the "layers upon layers of reality."[67]

Herzog's previously misguided intensity also accounts for the most highly praised feature of the novel. In his desperate effort "to explain, to have it out, to justify, to put into perspective, to clarify, to make amends"[68] and in his desire to relate everything to himself, Herzog pours his mind and soul into a series of aphorisms, letters, and fragmentary notes, that are never mailed. In addition to a few people that played a sad role in the breakup of his second marriage, he writes to long-abandoned loves, to eighteenth- and nineteenth-century philosophers, to dead friends and relatives, to God and occasionally to himself, revealing in these often involuntarily scribbled lines that seem dictated to him the wealth of his wit and the depth of his personality. Herzog's consciousness is a verbal one, and language is his means of grasping what is happening to him. Thus remembered pain and injustice throw him into a frenzy of writing:

> Quickly, quickly, more! The train rushed over the landscape. It swooped past New Haven. It ran with all its might toward Rhode Island. Herzog, now barely looking through the tinted, immovable, sealed window, felt his eager, flying spirit streaming out, speaking, piercing, making clear judgments, uttering final explanations, necessary words only. He was in a whirling ecstasy.[69]

Herzog does, however, also employ this eccentric compulsion of his to avoid facing reality. His version of the real is a verbal version and thus reductive: "I go after reality with language. Perhaps I'd like to change it all into language."[70] By and by, when his energy is almost spent, he comes to realize that the verbal environments he has created are only *ersatz*, meager substitutes for the real

thing: "I put my whole heart into these constructions. But they are constructions."[71] When peace
finally comes to him, his belligerent voice, like that
of Henderson, ceases to be heard. In the state of
equilibrium Herzog has no more letters to write,
no more messages to send to anyone.

Herzog's verbal ecstasy leads to the unusual
and highly effective changes in narrative perspective that depend on Herzog's momentary relation
to his former selves: "he" indicates attempts at objectivity or clarification, "I," strong identification
or the reexperiencing of an overpowering emotion.[72] It is understandable that Bellow maintains
that the form of this novel came into being during
the process of writing. The fanatic care he professes to have employed for the book—it is the result of fifteen versions[73]—has helped to fashion
Herzog into an absorbing piece of verbal reality
that, by its energy and commitment, transcends
construction to become art.

Bellow's only full-length play, *The Last Analysis* (1964), deals with the relativity and subjectiv-
ity of truth. The comedian Bummidge, a large,
stout man in his late fifties whose popularity has
been steadily decreasing, has resolved to give up
his activity as entertainer. He now has a message
to convey to mankind: he firmly believes that man
can experience a complete renewal by psychoanalytic means. He is willing to let psychiatrists
witness the process of his rebirth, which he hopes

to achieve by reliving the crucial episodes of his
life, starting with his birth. When Bummidge carries his project through, his intention to help
people suffering from depression like himself is
completely misunderstood. Without his knowledge, impresarios and "sponsors" have been allowed to watch Bummidge, at the side of members of
the American Psychiatric Association. While he
undergoes his autotherapeutic "Existenz-Action-
Self-Analysis" the unexpected happens on two levels. The sponsors are so taken by what they consider
Bummidge's "performance" that they anticipate a
magnificent comeback for him and offer him con-
tracts under his own conditions. But Bummidge
hardly recognizes them, nor is he interested in what
they offer him. Through having symbolically undergone birth, death, and rebirth, he has indeed become
a new man about to start a new life. Bellow himself
confirms this: "Our comedian Bummidge does
manage to burst the bonds of metaphor by certain
peculiar means, to 'get off the couch,' to stand on
his own feet, and even to dance a bit."[74]

Of course, Bummidge's seriousness is meant
to be part of the farce. The subject of the play, as
Bellow has pointed out in the introduction he
wrote for the publication of the play, "is the mind's
comical struggle for survival in an environment of
Ideas . . . and the peculiarly literal and solemn
manner in which Americans dedicate themselves
to programs, fancies, or brainstorms."[75]

Especially in the ideas presented, the two-act

play is closely related to Bellow's other works. In it Bellow seems to have attempted a literalization of the metaphors of theatricality in *Herzog*. All the main figures in *Herzog* are at one time or other directly called actors; there is much talk about putting on shows, changing roles, performing, and clowning. The characterization of Madeleine as an impresario's daughter contains some rich examples of this mock-dramatic mode, in which the irony shows beneath the genealogy. With his vivid visual gifts Herzog occasionally invents fantastic imaginary "backdrops" as settings for the ranting of his emotions.[76] The motto, formulated by Herzog, that "civilized intelligence makes fun of its own ideas"[77] could be inscribed in both *The Last Analysis* and *Herzog*. Moses Herzog and Philip Bummidge both belong to the category of "that suffering joker."[78] Finally, Bummidge, the clown who has just made a comeback in a different line of work, refuses, like Herzog, to play any more roles.

Various further similarities pertain not only to *Herzog* but to other protagonists of Bellow's novels as well. History, memory, and the knowledge of death as the catalysts that transform us into true human beings function as such not only in *Herzog* but in *Augie March* and *Henderson* as well. Part of their transforming power is shown on stage in *The Last Analysis*. Bummidge, like Henderson, is on an expedition for truth.[79] He suffers from the queer disease of Humanitis—"when the human condition is suddenly too much for you"[80]

—of which Henderson also complains.[81] Like Henderson, he is going through a process of rebirth that in his case is achieved not on the mythic but on the psychoanalytic level. Like Augie, like Henderson and very much like Herzog, he feels that the enterprise he has set out to undertake is "bigger than me, but there's nobody else to do it."[82] The "universal significance"[83] of his project weighs him down. Having escaped treacherous plots by greedy relatives and managers, the tangle of his own confused mind, and the overpowering impact of his past, Bummidge seeks a meaningful life by trying to serve others.

Bummidge is allowed to do on stage what Herzog only "acts out" in his mind: he relives his past life. On his quest for purification and for truth about the self, Bummidge succumbs to "ideas" and "metaphors." He makes Freudian psychoanalysis—which Bellow has elsewhere called a system of metaphors[84]—his means to salvation.

When the play was first produced in 1964 at the Belasco Theater in New York, it was not a success. Bellow revised heavily and published the new version a few months later. The reason for the play's failure may well lie in this mixture of comedy and seriousness. The seriousness mocks itself, but one is never quite sure to what degree or extent. Bummidge's rebirth cannot be taken by the audience for what he himself takes it; if so, the playgoers could be accused of having missed the satire. On the other hand, Bummidge's aspirations are too great, the subject of the play too serious, to be treated only farcically.

Confusion, as Bummidge's wife aptly complains in a context of her own, here also seems to manifest itself as the fruit of originality.[85] What remains to be pondered is whether the energy that gets Bummidge off the couch is the same kind of energy that Herzog is depending on to keep him permanently out of his hammock.

6

The Benefit

of an

Enlarged

Vision

I n *Mr. Sammler's Planet* Bellow's mind orbits
steadily around the basic concerns of his work.
The novel not only takes up the old concepts but
repeats previous formulations as well. The "change
of the heart," the "new conduct,"[1] the "true nature
of human beings,"[2] are all sounded again and given
new intensity through their echoing quality. Coming from Mr. Artur Sammler they are especially
impressive, as foreign-born, Polish-Oxonian Sammler is hardly given to expressing his personal
views on philosophical questions. A septuagenar-
ian, a Jew, a European immigrant, he has led a
truly varied life that has taught him the virtue of
silence. Yet he is not so completely detached and
aloof as he would like to be but is torn between disinterestedness and the seemingly inescapable attraction of life. His eyesight is a metaphor for his state
of mind. One eye has been blinded through a blow
with a gun butt; this damaged eye "seemed to
turn in another direction, to be preoccupied sep-
arately with different matters."[3] He has not become
immune to certain types of distraction.

Sammler criticizes his own lack of immunity
rather severely. As a man who has been counted as
dead he believes he should be perfectly free from
all interests, "released from Nature, from impressions, and from everyday life,"[4] and, most of all,
from memories and their tormenting onrush. Sammler has led a cosmopolitan life. He grew up in

Cracow before World War I and spent the 1920s and 1930s as the London correspondent of some eastern-European newspapers. During that time he was acquainted with members of the Bloomsbury group, especially H. G. Wells, on whom he considers writing a book. He was on a visit to Poland when it was invaded by Nazi Germany. His wife was killed in the mass execution that he miraculously survived. Or, as it seems in his eyes, he merely "lasted," not survived. Sammler makes this distinction to reject both praise and blame for still being on this earth. After his escape from death he was reduced to a less-than-human state, having been driven to near insanity by the hardships he had to undergo in order to survive. Once he killed a German soldier and, in his depravity, experienced a sudden pleasure in it and even longed to "drink more flames."[5] Half-starved and clad in rags, he and his daughter Shula finally reached the displaced-persons camp at Salzburg. From there, his wife's nephew, Dr. Elya Gruner, rescued them in 1947 and brought them to New York.

Sammler now lives in his niece Margotte's apartment on the Upper West side in Manhattan, pursuing fervidly his mental occupation: trying to come to terms with the past, with life in New York, with the possibility of mankind's leaving this earth for the moon. "Wasn't it the time, the very hour to go?," he asks himself, referring to space travel as well as to that other journey into the unknown. But Sammler also recognizes the strong centripetal power of life: "One was always, and so powerfully, so persuasively, drawn back to human conditions."[6]

The irony of the present action—which is again, as in *Herzog*, compressed into a few days—lies in the fact that Sammler once again finds death too fleet of foot for him. This time, it is Elya Gruner who is dying. By a series of seemingly "deliberate" incidents, among which are a lecture by Sammler at Columbia University that is disrupted by radicals, a most disturbing encounter with a Negro pickpocket, who notices that Sammler has observed him at work, the tracking down of an irreplaceable manuscript that was taken from the rightful owner by Shula, Sammler is prevented from doing the one thing he really wants to do: to see his benefactor Elya once more before Elya dies. The clutter of circumstances that is a vivid illustration of what "distraction" can do intercepts him effectively. When he reaches the hospital, Elya is dead.

Thus the span of the novel's action comprises the time it takes for a man to die. Sammler's increasing awareness of the inevitable forces him to acknowledge an inborn "natural knowledge" that lies beyond words: "The terms which, in his inmost heart, each man knows. As I know mine. As all know."[7] The soul of man he imagines as sitting "unhappily on superstructures of explanations, poor bird, not knowing which way to fly."[8] The recognition of the futility of explanations is one of Sammler's basic insights. He once considered himself something of a historian of civilization and, through his work as journalist, an instructor of the masses. With his haughty, snobbish, not altogether charitable character, he might formerly have embodied one of Bellow's reality instructors. His social, economic, and for a time even human descent, however, demonstrated to him the imprecision of the historical outlook and the impossibility of the synthesis of all facts. This sense that man is doomed to having to cope with a mind that must helplessly watch its categories continually being upset is intensified by what Sammler refers to as the "madness" of life in contemporary New York:

> The many impressions and experiences of life seemed no longer to occur each in its own proper space, in sequence, each with its recognizable religious or aesthetic importance, but human beings suffered the humiliations of inconsequence, of confused styles, of a long life containing several separate lives. In fact the whole experience of mankind was now covering each separate life in its flood. Making all the ages of history simultaneous. Compelling the frail person to receive, to register, depriving him because of volume, of mass, of the power to impart design.[9]

Thus explanations, attempted by a confused species, can lead only to other versions of fiction, not to reality.[10]

The "absurd craving" for coherency that is inherent to man can neither be stilled nor fulfilled. Instead of trying to find reasons for everything, one should rather attempt to draw distinctions in

order to do justice to life's phenomena: "One had
to learn to distinguish. To distinguish and distinguish and distinguish. It was distinguishing, not
explanation, that mattered. Explanation was for
the mental masses . . . But distinguishing? A
higher activity."[11] Overcome by "the inadequacy
of words," Sammler has changed, among other
things, his reading habits. The only profitable
reading he now finds are the works of the thir-
teenth-century German mystics—Suso, Tauler,
Meister Eckhart. He has become a "specialist in
short views,"[12] and they are very much his own,
diverging considerably from the generally accepted
standards. Like Herzog, who no longer considers
himself a scholar and critic, Sammler feels himself
incapable of writing the book he had planned on
H. G. Wells. Writing it would surely involve judging. And to avoid judgment has become a measure
of Sammler's increased humanity: "The best, I
have found, is to be disinterested. Not as misan-
thropes dissociate themselves, by judging, but by
not judging."[13]

This vow of disinterestedness, from which,
however, he has occasional lapses, explains the
quality of remoteness that characterizes Sammler.
He feels himself "somewhat separated from the
rest of the species, if not in some fashion severed,"[14]
a "visiting consciousness,"[15] an outsider by choice.
Because of his knowledge of the past, because of
his old-world civility that makes him at least out-
wardly a patient listener, because of his equanimity

and objectivity, Sammler is at all times being visited by people who consult him and confess to him. Often such a confession, as, for example, those offered by his promiscuous niece Angela Gruner, is really an attempt on the part of the visitor to correct an unflattering self-image by obtaining some kind of justification from Sammler. He is known for giving his attention to all sides, for attending to important and small matters with equal fairness and kindness. He collects people around him; he is "their Sammler,"[16] as Bellow points out in his pun on the German meaning of the name (*Sammler* means collector).

Among those who flock to him are students and ex-students, Margotte and Angela, Angela's brother Wallace. Most of all, there is his daughter Shula—Shula approaching forty, who has adopted eccentricity and bohemianism to make herself an object of attention and, hopefully, of love, who steals a manuscript containing the latest information on the moon because she believes it will help her father with his H. G. Wells project. To all of them, Sammler listens, feeling that "inside him was a field in which many hunters at cross purposes were firing bird shot at a feather apparition assumed to be a bird."[17] Unable to influence the madness, the craving, the insatiable needs he is confronted with, he merely registers, observes, and consciously enjoys the states of heightened perception that are achieved especially through unpleasant and disturbing events or through downright

evil. When the masterful pickpocket wordlessly ex-
poses his genitals to Sammler, Sammler is overcome
by this act as a demonstration of sovereignty: "It
was a mystery. It was unanswerable. The whole explanation."[18] Sammler the sage manages to translate humiliation and repulsion into illumination.
He receives "the benefit of an enlarged vision."[19]

With his objectivity, however, he is critical of
the "theatricality in people,"[20] of the exaggeration
of their own importance that drives them to make
limitless demands on life. The central demand he
recognizes as the refusal "to go away from this
earth unsatisfied."[21] Dissatisfied people, especially
the young, act without dignity. In the midst of all
this Sammler tries to perform a kind of symbolic
task because he is "a Sammler"[22] and being a Sammler puts him under an obligation. Under such an
obligation he passes on his "short views": One must
try "to live with a civil heart. With disinterested
charity"[23]; one must do one's duty, do what is re-
quired of one; most of all, one must strive for
order, beginning with the order within oneself.
This, he says, is "better than what many call love.
Perhaps it *is* love."[24] Thus Sammler opens his heart
in a long conversation with Dr. Govinda Lal, the
author of the stolen manuscript, which is finally
retrieved from Shula. Sammler is by no means opposed to the prospect of cultivating the moon, as it
may force people to concern themselves with only
the basic questions again.[25] Personally, he is content to sit in his West Side apartment and watch

"those gorgeous Faustian departures for the other worlds."[26] The idea of infinite space makes him somewhat uncomfortable; he "requires a ceiling."[27] He is kept busy enough trying to achieve "non-intimidation by doom."[28]

The question of whether the imagination has been able to produce "a human figure of adequate stature"[29] is answered negatively in the book. Several critics feel the same about Mr. Sammler as a character and have attacked his personality for betraying a feeling of superiority toward all figures except Elya Gruner. This impression is partly the result of technique: it arises through Sammler's almost uninterrupted flow of mental comments, by which he tries to achieve perspective. Bellow seems to have been pursued by the image of the prototype of Mr. Sammler, whom he saw in Paris years ago: "He was an old half-Russian, half-Italian who spent the war hiding in France. He had Mr. Sammler's appearance, his blindness, his walk. Some people come back like Hecuba. They are nothing to me. I am nothing to them. But they are the most important people in my life."[30]

It is, however, interesting to note that Bellow should choose such a remote and other-worldly character as his persona. Perhaps it was Sammler's perspective on contemporary America that Bellow wanted to make use of. Here was a man who had seen the worst and yet managed to retain dignity; a meticulous observer who upheld kindness; a knowledgeable man who suspended judgment; and

and a sensitive man who defined love as order.
Through Sammler's age and the quality of experience that adheres to his person, Bellow could
—in Sammler's words—convert pain and suffering
"into delicate, even piercing observation."[31] In the
figure of Sammler he found a means of uniting
paradoxical qualities, of creating a plausible if
somewhat elegiac equanimity. Sammler's remoteness, moreover, structurally balances the fact that
he is the one main character of the book; his presence is felt, but not obtrusively.

Sammler's trained, elegant mind is reflected
in the style, the precision of which is unrivaled by
any other of Bellow's novels. The language of *Mr.
Sammler's Planet* surpasses that of *Herzog* through
this very brevity. It is marked by gentle wit and an
admirable control of the emotions.

It is difficult to imagine where Bellow will go
from here. The development that is clearly recog-
nizable throughout his work concerns not only
language and characterization but also the approach to the form of the novel. As the characters
grow older, more mature, and more "human"—a
term that means to Bellow an increasing awareness
and appreciation of the qualities that enable the
individual as well as mankind to "survive"—the
language becomes more controlled, more concise,
more elegant, with greater emphasis being placed
on the subliminal emotional content of each single
word. As is natural in this context, the joyfulness
and exuberance, the undauntable love of life that

characterized *Augie March* and *Henderson*, gradually diminish.

This is also the result of the growing importance of ideas in Bellow's later work. Remembering, evaluating, imagining, and reinterpreting become the protagonists' main "business" in life, a development that clearly indicates Bellow's changing attitude toward the novel. Artistic self-expression has become of secondary importance compared to the unending stream-of-thought processes contained in *Herzog* and *Mr. Sammler's Planet.* These novels are not only the comprehensive records that "compulsive witnesses" of their own lives have taken down, they also represent Bellow's effort to turn the novel into a medium of inquiry. In Bellow's most recent novels, experiences are not so much being undergone as discussed in a probing approach that may well be called essayistic. More and more is being asked of the protagonists as characters. They are not merely reborn once as, for instance, Bummidge or Tommy Wilhelm were, but, through the circumstances of the contemporary world, are forced to lead three or four different lives the way Sammler was. Thus the demands made on their mental capacities to cope with this flood of events and perceptions increases proportionately. It leads to the near exclusion of action and real dialogue in favor of reflection and a steadily lessening desire for communication. The long stretches of almost audible quietness that pervades the room in which Sammler does most of his thinking may be indicative of Bellow's present inclination for the "nonfiction philosophical novel" as well as his modification of a literature courting silence. The chain may lead from shouting to speaking to thinking to merely "being," a term that is given special emphasis in as early a novel as *Augie March*. What consequences this will have for Bellow's novels remains to be seen. His own attitude toward his further writing appears to be a mixture of seeming naiveté, real curiosity, and cautious optimism: "I am just a man in the position of waiting to see what the imagination is going to do next."[32]

Notes

Introduction

1. Norman Mailer, "Some Children of the Goddess," in *Cannibals and Christians*, New York, 1966, p. 127.
2. Clayton, p. 3.
3. T. Tanner, *Saul Bellow*, p. 111.
4. Alexandre Maurocordato, *Les quatre dimensions du Herzog de Saul Bellow*, Paris, 1969.
5. H. Harper, *Desperate Faith*, p. 64.
6. J. Baumbach, *The Landscape of Nightmare*, p. 54.
7. N. Scott, *Adversity and Grace*, p. 30.
8. N. Scott, *Adversity and Grace*, p. 30.
9. G. Harper, "The Art of Fiction," pp. 52ff.
10. Clayton, p. 5.
11. *Time*, 9 Feb. 1970, p. 82.
12. N. Steers, "Successor to Faulkner?" p. 37.
13. Bellow, as quoted in *Twentieth Century Authors*, p. 72.
14. Bellow, "Laughter in the Ghetto," *Saturday Review of Literature* 36, 30 May 1953, p. 15.
15. N. Steers, "Successor to Faulkner?" p. 37.
16. Bellow, "Distractions of a Fiction Writer," p. 2f.

1. The Price of Release

1. G. Harper, "The Art of Fiction," p. 56.
2. *Dangling Man*, p. 84.
3. *Dangling Man*, p. 9.
4. *Dangling Man*, p. 11.
5. *Dangling Man*, p. 18.
6. *Dangling Man*, p. 191.
7. *Dangling Man*, p. 151.
8. *Dangling Man*, p. 39.
9. *Dangling Man*, p. 57.
10. *Dangling Man*, p. 9.
11. *Dangling Man*, p. 27.
12. *Dangling Man*, p. 174.
13. *Dangling Man*, p. 91.
14. *Dangling Man*, p. 39.
15. *Dangling Man*, p. 84.
16. *Dangling Man*, p. 13.
17. *Dangling Man*, p. 24f.
18. *Dangling Man*, p. 118f.
19. *Dangling Man*, p. 137.
20. *Dangling Man*, p. 92.
21. *Dangling Man*, p. 82.
22. *Dangling Man*, p. 28.
23. *Dangling Man*, p. 154.
24. G. Harper, "The Art of Fiction," p. 56.
25. *The Victim*, p. 20.
26. *The Victim*, p. 274.
27. *The Victim*, p. 29.
28. *The Victim*, p. 38.
29. *The Victim*, pp. 208, 271.
30. *The Victim*, p. 158.
31. *The Victim*, p. 94.
32. *The Victim*, p. 154.
33. *The Victim*, p. 219.
34. *The Victim*, p. 51.
35. *The Victim*, p. 146.

36. *The Victim*, p. 264.
37. *The Victim*, p. 183f.
38. *The Victim*, p. 64.
39. *The Victim*, p. 3.
40. *The Victim*, p. 257f.
41. *The Victim*, p. 169.
42. *The Victim*, p. 98.
43. *The Victim*, p. 179.
44. *The Victim*, p. 255.
45. *The Victim*, p. 133.
46. *The Victim*, p. 134.
47. *The Victim*, p. 133.
48. G. Harper, "The Art of Fiction," p. 55.
49. G. Harper, "The Art of Fiction," p. 56.
50. G. Harper, "The Art of Fiction," p. 58.

2. Bitterness in His Chosen Thing

1. Harvey Breit, "Talk with Saul Bellow," p. 22.
2. Bellow, "The Trip to Galena," p. 782.
3. Bellow, "The Trip to Galena," p. 789.
4. *The Adventures of Augie March*, p. 491.
5. Bellow, as quoted in *Twentieth Century Authors*, p. 73.
6. *Augie March*, p. 327.
7. *Augie March*, p. 491.
8. *Augie March*, p. 444.
9. Bellow, as quoted in *Twentieth Century Authors*, p. 72.
10. *Augie March*, p. 7.
11. *Augie March*, p. 9.
12. *Augie March*, p. 15.
13. *Augie March*, p. 36.
14. *Augie March*, p. 35.
15. *Augie March*, p. 76.
16. *Augie March*, p. 83.

17. *Augie March*, p. 134f.
18. *Augie March*, p. 97.
19. *Augie March*, p. 144f.
20. *Augie March*, p. 175.
21. *Augie March*, p. 183.
22. *Augie March*, p. 260.
23. *Augie March*, p. 376f.
24. *Augie March*, p. 470.
25. *Augie March*, p. 465.
26. *Augie March*, p. 450.
27. *Augie March*, p. 398.
28. *Augie March*, p. 361.
29. *Augie March*, p. 456.
30. *Augie March*, p. 462.
31. *Augie March*, p. 582.
32. *Augie March*, p. 607.
33. *Augie March*, p. 482.
34. Bellow, "Distractions of a Fiction Writer," p. 3.
35. Bellow, "Address by Gooley MacDowell to the Has-
    beens Club of Chicago," p. 226.
36. *Augie March*, p. 273.
37. *Augie March,* p. 516.
38. *Augie March*, p. 450.
39. *Augie March*, p. 510.
40. *Augie March*, p. 274.
41. *Augie March*, p. 511.
42. *Augie March*, p. 502.
43. Bellow, "A Sermon by Dr. Pep," p. 460.
44. *Augie March*, p. 70.
45. *Augie March*, p. 87.
46. *Augie March*, p. 494.
47. *Augie March*, p. 435.
48. *Augie March*, p. 473.
49. *Augie March*, p. 88.
50. *Augie March*, p. 520.
51. *Augie March*, p. 237.
52. *Augie March*, p. 210.

53. Bellow, "Address by Gooley MacDowell to the Hasbeens Club of Chicago," p. 227.
54. *Augie March*, p. 373.
55. *Augie March*, p. 373.
56. *Augie March*, p. 515.
57. *Augie March*, p. 157.
58. *Augie March*, p. 286.
59. *Augie March*, p. 231.
60. Bellow, "Distractions of a Fiction Writer," p. 20.
61. Bellow, "How I Wrote Augie March's Story," p. 3.
62. *Augie March*, p. 510.

3. The Dread Is Great, The Soul Is Small

1. David Boroff, "The Author," *Saturday Review of Literature* 47, 19 Sept. 1964, p. 39.
2. Bellow, "Distractions of a Fiction Writer," p. 6.
3. Bellow, "Where Do We Go from Here: The Future of Fiction," pp. 27–33.
4. Bellow, "Distractions of a Fiction Writer," p. 15.
5. Bellow, "Where Do We Go from Here: The Future of Fiction," p. 30.
6. Bellow, "The Mexican General," 1942.
7. *Seize the Day*, p. 58.
8. *Seize the Day*, p. 115.
9. *Seize the Day*, p. 83.
10. *Seize the Day*, p. 61.
11. *Seize the Day*, p. 39.
12. *Seize the Day*, p. 10.
13. *Seize the Day,* p. 69.
14. *Seize the Day*, p. 98.
15. *Seize the Day*, p. 72.
16. *Seize the Day*, p. 57.
17. *Seize the Day*, p. 66.
18. *Seize the Day*, p. 93.
19. *Seize the Day*, p. 84f.

20. *Seize the Day*, p. 56.
21. *Seize the Day*, p. 14f.
22. *Seize the Day*, p. 14.
23. *Seize the Day*, p. 31.
24. *Seize the Day*, p. 84.
25. Tony Tanner, *Saul Bellow*, pp. 59ff.
26. *Seize the Day*, p. 129.
27. *Seize the Day*, p. 132.
28. *The Wrecker*, p. 211.
29. *A Wen*, p. 111.

4. Every Guy Has His Own Africa

1. *Henderson the Rain King*, p. 73.
2. *Henderson*, p. 73.
3. Bellow, "Deep Readers of the World, Beware!" p. 1.
4. Bellow, "Some Notes on Recent American Fiction,"
   p. 25.
5. Bellow, "Some Notes on Recent American Fiction,"
   p. 25.
6. *Augie March*, p. 550.
7. *Henderson*, p. 128.
8. *Henderson*, p. 89.
9. *Henderson*, p. 180.
10. *Henderson*, p. 244.
11. *Henderson*, p. 24.
12. *Henderson*, p. 251.
13. *Henderson*, p. 20.
14. *Henderson*, p. 9.
15. Several critics have pointed out the spoken, conver-
    sational quality of Bellow's language, e.g. Earl Rovit,
    Saul Bellow, p. 42.
16. *Henderson*, p. 270.
17. *Henderson*, p. 288.
18. N. Steers, "Successor to Faulkner?" p. 38.
19. *Henderson*, p. 205.

20. *Henderson*, p. 159.
21. *Henderson*, p. 99.
22. *Henderson*, p. 266.
23. *Henderson*, p. 255.
24. *Henderson*, p. 253.
25. *Henderson*, p. 255.
26. *Henderson*, p. 166f.
27. N. Steers, "Successor to Faulkner?" p. 38.
28. *Henderson*, p. 177.
29. G. Harper, "The Art of Fiction," p. 70.

5. History, Memory—That Is What Makes Us Human

1. *Herzog*, p. 203.
2. D. Boroff, "The Author," *Saturday Review of Literature* 47, 19 Sept. 1964, p. 39.
3. D. Boroff, "The Author," p. 38.
4. *Herzog*, p. 148.
5. N. Steers, "Successor to Faulkner?" p. 36f.
6. *Herzog*, p. 155.
7. N. Steers, "Successor to Faulkner?" p. 37.
8. *Herzog*, p. 285; N. Steers, "Successor to Faulkner?" p. 38.
9. G. Harper, "The Art of Fiction," p. 56.
10. *Herzog*, p. 244; Bellow, "The Jewish Writer and the English Literary Tradition," p. 366.
11. *Herzog*, p. 191.
12. *Herzog*, p. 17.
13. *Herzog*, p. 9.
14. *Herzog*, p. 156.
15. G. Harper, "The Art of Fiction," p. 70.
16. *Herzog*, p. 134.
17. *Herzog*, p. 80.
18. *Herzog*, p. 84.
19. *Herzog*, p. 83.
20. *Herzog*, p. 174f.

21. *Herzog*, p. 127.
22. *Herzog*, p. 47.
23. *Herzog*, p. 175.
24. *Herzog*, p. 173.
25. *Herzog*, p. 19.
26. *Herzog*, p. 63.
27. *Herzog*, p. 41.
28. *Herzog*, p. 275.
29. *Herzog*, p. 176.
30. *Herzog*, p. 314.
31. *Herzog*, p. 283.
32. *Herzog*, p. 332.
33. *Herzog*, p. 13.
34. Bellow, "Two Faces of a Hostile World," *New York Times Book Review*, 26 Aug. 1956, p. 5.
35. Bellow, "The Writer as Moralist," p. 61.
36. Bellow, "A Comment on 'Form and Despair,'" p. 10.
37. Bellow, "Where Do We Go from Here: The Future of Fiction," p. 30.
38. Bellow, "A Word from Writer Directly to Reader," in: *Fiction of the Fifties*, ed. Herbert Gold, New York, 1959, p. 19.
39. Bellow, "Where Do We Go from Here: The Future of Fiction," p. 33.
40. Especially Richard Poirier, "Bellows to Herzog," p. 271.
41. G. Harper, "The Art of Fiction," p. 71.
42. G. Harper, "The Art of Fiction," p. 69.
43. *Herzog*, p. 113.
44. *Herzog*, p. 57.
45. *Herzog*, p. 101.
46. *Herzog*, p. 157.
47. *Herzog*, p. 200.
48. *Herzog*, p. 212.
49. *Herzog*, p. 163.

50. *Herzog*, p. 202.
51. D. Boroff, "The Author," p. 38.
52. G. Harper, "The Art of Fiction," p. 62.
53. *Herzog*, p. 90.
54. *Herzog*, p. 205.
55. *Herzog*, p. 83.
56. *Herzog*, p. 178.
57. *Herzog*, p. 228.
58. *Herzog*, p. 351.
59. *Herzog*, p. 100.
60. G. Harper, "The Art of Fiction," p. 67.
61. Bellow, "The Writer as Moralist," p. 62.
62. *Herzog*, pp. 35, 288.
63. *Herzog*, p. 25.
64. *Herzog*, p. 12.
65. *Herzog*, p. 299f.
66. *Herzog*, p. 336.
67. *Herzog*, p. 117.
68. *Herzog*, p. 10.
69. *Herzog*, p. 76.
70. *Herzog*, p. 283.
71. *Herzog*, p. 283.
72. *Herzog*, pp. 242ff.
73. D. Boroff, "The Author," p. 39.
74. "My Man Bummidge," p. 5.
75. *The Last Analysis*, p. 7.
76. *Herzog*, p. 184.
77. *Herzog*, p. 282.
78. *Herzog*, p. 19.
79. *The Last Analysis*, p. 18.
80. *The Last Analysis*, p. 41.
81. *Henderson the Rain King*, p. 41.
82. *The Last Analysis*, p. 15.
83. *The Last Analysis*, p. 7.
84. D. Boroff, "The Author," p. 38.
85. *The Last Analysis*, p. 61.

6.   The Benefit of an Enlarged Vision

1. *Mr. Sammler's Planet,* p. 287.
2. *Sammler,* p. 236.
3. *Sammler,* p. 35.
4. *Sammler,* p. 121.
5. *Sammler,* p. 144.
6. *Sammler,* p. 121.
7. *Sammler,* p. 316.
8. *Sammler,* p. 7.
9. *Sammler,* p. 30.
10. *Sammler,* p. 22.
11. *Sammler,* p. 67.
12. *Sammler,* p. 167.
13. *Sammler,* p. 239.
14. *Sammler,* p. 47.
15. *Sammler,* p. 77.
16. *Sammler,* p. 269.
17. *Sammler,* p. 202.
18. *Sammler,* p. 59.
19. *Sammler,* p. 15.
20. *Sammler,* p. 234.
21. *Sammler,* p. 38.
22. *Sammler,* p. 118.
23. *Sammler,* p. 140.
24. *Sammler,* p. 231.
25. *Sammler,* p. 57.
26. *Sammler,* p. 187.
27. *Sammler,* p. 187.
28. *Sammler,* p. 138.
29. *Sammler,* p. 236.
30. Martha Duffy, Interview with Saul Bellow, *Time,* 9 Feb. 1970, p. 82.
31. *Sammler,* p. 48.
32. N. Steers, "Successor to Faulkner?" p. 38.

Bibliography

Works by Saul Bellow

"Address by Gooley MacDowell to the Hasbeens Club of Chicago." *Hudson Review* 4(1951):222–27.

The Adventures of Augie March. New York: Viking Press, 1953.

"By the Rock Wall." *Harper's Bazaar*, 85, April 1951, pp. 135ff.

"A Comment on 'Form and Despair.'" *Location* 1(1964): 10–12.

Dangling Man. New York: Vanguard, 1944.

"Deep Readers of the World, Beware!" *New York Times Book Review*, 15 February 1959, pp. 1, 34.

"Distractions of a Fiction Writer." In *The Living Novel,* edited by G. Hicks, pp. 1–20. New York, 1957.

"Dora." *Harper's Bazaar* 83, November 1949, pp. 118, 188–90, 198–99.

"Facts That Put Fancy to Flight." *New York Times Book Review*, 11 February 1962, pp. 1, 28.

Henderson the Rain King. New York: Viking Press, 1959.

Herzog. New York: Viking Press, 1964.

"How I Wrote Augie March's Story." *New York Times Book Review*, 31 January 1954, pp. 3, 17.

"The Jewish Writer and the English Literary Tradition." *Commentary* 8(1949):366–67.

The Last Analysis. New York: Viking Press, 1965.

"Literature." In *Great Ideas Today,* pp. 135–79. New York, 1963.

"The Mexican General." *Partisan Review* 9(1942):178–94.

Mr. Sammler's Planet. New York: Viking Press, 1970.

Mosby's Memoirs. New York: Viking Press, 1968.

"My Man Bummidge." *New York Times,* 27 September 1964, Section 2, p. 1.

"The Sealed Treasure." *Times Literary Supplement,* 1 July 1960, p. 414.

Seize the Day. New York: Viking Press, 1956.

"A Sermon by Dr. Pep." *Partisan Review* 16(1949):455–62.

"Skepticism and the Depth of Life." In *The Arts and the Public,* edited by J. E. Miller and P. D. Herring, pp. 13–30. Chicago, 1967.

"Some Notes on Recent American Fiction." *Encounter* 21 (1963):22–29.

"Thinking Man's Waste Land." *Saturday Review of Literature* 48, 3 April 1965, p. 20.

"The Trip to Galena." *Partisan Review* 17(1950):769–94.

"Two Morning Monologues." *Partisan Review* 8(1941):230–36.

"The University as Villain." *The Nation* 185, 16 November 1957, pp. 361–63.

The Victim. New York: Vanguard, 1947.

A Wen. Esquire, January 1965, pp. 72–74, 111.

"Where Do We Go from Here: The Future of Fiction." *Michigan Quarterly Review* 1(1962):27–33.

"The Writer as Moralist." *Atlantic Monthly* 211(1963):58–62.

Works about Saul Bellow

Baumbach, Jonathan. "The Double Vision: *The Victim* by Saul Bellow." In *The Landscape of Nightmare,* pp. 35–54. New York, 1965.

Bezanker, Abraham. "The Odyssey of Saul Bellow." *Yale Review* 58(1969):359–71.

Boroff, David. "Saul Bellow." *Saturday Review of Literature* 47, 19 September 1964, pp. 38–39, 77.

Breit, Harvey. "Talk with Saul Bellow." *New York Times Book Review*, 20 September 1953, p. 22.

Clayton, John J. *Saul Bellow: In Defense of Man*. Bloomington, Indiana, 1968.

Crozier, Robert D. "Theme in *Augie March*." *Critique* 7 (1965):18–32.

Davis, Robert Gorham. "The American Individualist Tradition: Bellow and Styron." In *The Creative Present*, edited by Nona Balakian and Charles Simmons, pp. 111–41. New York, 1963.

Demarest, David. "The Theme of Discontinuity in Saul Bellow's Fiction." *Studies in Short Fiction* 6(1969):175–86.

Detweiler, Robert. "Patterns of Rebirth in *Henderson*." *Modern Fiction Studies* 12(1966):405–14.

Dickstein, Morris. "For Art's Sake." *Partisan Review* 33 (1966):617–21.

Dommergues, Pierre. *Saul Bellow*. Paris, 1967.

Donoghue, Denis. "Commitment and the Dangling Man." *Studies* 53(1964):174–87.

Enck, John. "Saul Bellow: An Interview." *Contemporary Literature* 6(1965):156–60.

Galloway, David. "An Interview with Saul Bellow." *Audit* 3(1963):19–23.

Galloway, David. "The Absurd Man as Picaro." In *The Absurd Hero in American Fiction*, pp. 82–139. Austin, Texas, and London, 1966.

Goldberg, Gerald J. "Life's Customer, Augie March." *Critique* 3(1960):15–27.

Guerard, Albert J. "Saul Bellow and the Activists." *Southern Review* 3(1967):582–96.

Gutwillig, Robert. "Talk with Saul Bellow." *New York Times Book Review*, 20 September 1964, p. 40.

Harper, Gordon L. "The Art of Fiction XXXVII: Saul Bellow." *Paris Review* 9(1966):48–73.

Harper, Howard M. "Saul Bellow—the Heart's Ultimate Need." In *Desperate Faith*, pp. 7–64. Chapel Hill, North Carolina, 1967.

Hassan, Ihab. "Saul Bellow: The Quest and Affirmation of Reality." In *Radical Innocence*, pp. 290–324. Princeton, New Jersey, 1961.

Kunitz, Stanley. "Saul Bellow." In *Twentieth Century Authors*, first supplement, pp. 72–73. New York, 1955.

Malin, Irving, ed. *Saul Bellow and the Critics*. New York, 1967.

Malin, Irving. *Saul Bellow's Fiction*. Carbondale, Illinois, 1969.

Mathis, James C. "The Theme of *Seize the Day*." *Critique* 7(1965):43–45.

Maurocordato, Alexandre. *Les quatre dimensions du Herzog de Saul Bellow*. Archiv des Lettres Modernes 102. Paris, 1969.

Morrow, Patrick. "Threat and Accommodation: The Novels of Saul Bellow." *Midwest Quarterly* 8(1967):389–411.

Opdahl, Keith M. *The Novels of Saul Bellow*. University Park, Pennsylvania, and London, 1967.

Poirier, Richard. "Bellows to Herzog." *Partisan Review* 32 (1965):264–71.

Rovit, Earl. *Saul Bellow*. University of Minnesota Press Pamphlets on American Writers 65. Minneapolis, 1967.

Rupp, Richard H. "Saul Bellow: Belonging to the World in General." In *Celebration in Postwar American Fiction 1945–1967*, pp. 189–208. Coral Gables, Florida, 1970.

Schneider, Harold W. "Two Bibliographies: Saul Bellow, William Styron." *Critique* 3(1960):71–91.

Schulz, Max F. "Saul Bellow and the Burden of Selfhood." In *Radical Sophistication*, pp. 110–53. Athens, Ohio, 1970.

Scott, Nathan A. "Sola Gratia: The Principle of Saul Bellow's Fiction." In *Adversity and Grace*, edited by N. A. Scott, pp. 27–57. Essays in Divinity 4. Chicago and London, 1968.

Shulman, Robert. "The Style of Bellow's Comedy." *Publications of the Modern Language Association* 83(1968): 109–117.

Steers, Nina. "Successor to Faulkner?" *Show* 4, September 1964, pp. 37–38.

Tanner, Tony. *Saul Bellow*. Edinburgh and London, 1965.
———. "Saul Bellow: The Flight from Monologue." *Encounter* 24(1965):58–70.

Weber, Ronald. "Bellow's Thinkers." *Western Humanities Review* 22(1968):305–313.

Young, James Dean. "Bellow's View of the Heart." *Critique* 7(1965):5–17.

Index

"Address by Gooley Mac-
    Dowell to the Has-
    beens Club of Chi-
    cago," 46–47, 53
  quoted, 47
Adler, Dr., *see* Dr. Adler
*Adventures of Augie March,
    The,* 4, 32, 33–56, 60,
    62, 79–80, 103, 113,
    127, 128
  as beginning of new Bel-
    low style, 29
  as *Bildungsroman,* 57–58
  picaresque elements in, 57
  quoted, 34, 37–39, 41–42,
    45, 47, 49, 52, 53–56
*Adventures of Huckleberry
    Finn, The* (Twain)
  *The Adventures of Augie
    March* and, 57
Africa in modern literature,
    79
Allbee, Kirby, *see* Kirby
    Allbee
Artur Sammler, 74, 118–26,
    127
  meaning of name, 123
Asa Leventhal, 17–28, 64–65

"Aspern Papers" (James)
  "The Gonzaga Manu-
    scripts" and, 71
Augie March, 33–56, 63–64,
    70, 79–80, 114
  opposition, quality of, 37–
    38, 39–40, 45, 51–52,
    54–55

"Bear, The" (Faulkner)
  Henderson the Rain King
    and, 80
Bellow, Saul
  attitudes toward literature
    and the novel, 5–6,
    56–57, 75, 102, 126–
    27, 128
  birth, 3
  childhood and youth, 3,
    35, 93
  defiance of philosophical
    pessimism, 3, 5, 92,
    101–102, 107–108 (*see
    also* themes)
  education, 4
  father, 3–4
  future developments in
    works, 126–28

heritage of varied background, influence on works, 3, 5

Jewish influence on works, 92, 93–94

languages, 5

mother, 4, 93

novel of ideas, as writer of, 127 (*see also* novel of ideas)

on his own writing, 28, 29–30, 60–61, 92, 93, 107–108, 128

on the power of imagination, 61–62, 78, 102 (*see also* themes)

on symbolism, 78–79

style in writing, 6, 29, 56–57, 60

teaching positions, ix, x, 4

travels in Europe, 4–5

"victim literature" and, 28, 105–106

W.P.A. writer's project and, 4

Bildungsroman
  The Adventures of Augie March as, 57–58
  Herzog as, 102–103

B'nai B'rith Jewish Heritage Award, x

Breit, Harvey, 57

Bummidge, Philip, *see* Philip Bummidge

Burroughs, William, 57

Camus, Albert
  influence on *The Victim*, 28

Catcher in the Rye, The (Salinger)
  The Adventures of Augie March and, 57

Chicago, Bellow's youth in, 3–4, 35, 93

Clayton, John, 2, 3

"Comment on 'Form and Despair,' A," 102

Committee on Social Thought, University of Chicago, Bellow as chairman of, 4

Confessions of an English Opium Eater, The (DeQuincey)
  quoted in *The Victim*, 18
  The Victim compared to, 25

Conrad, Joseph, 79

Crab and the Butterfly, The (not extant), 32

critics, the, general comments of
  on *The Adventures of Augie March*, 51
  on Bellow's total work, 2–3
  on *Henderson the Rain King*, 88–89
  on *Herzog*, 102–103, 106
  on *Mr. Sammler's Planet*, 125

Croix de Chevalier des Arts et Lettres, x

Dahfu, *see* King Dahfu

Dangling Man, 4, 8–17, 28, 37, 56–57, 60, 62, 68
  quoted, 10, 13–14, 17

DeQuincey, Thomas
  quoted in *The Victims*, 18

"Distractions of a Fiction Writer"
  quoted, 46, 61–62

Dr. Adler, 62–71

Dr. Tamkin, 62–71

Donne, John
  works of, and *The Adven-
    tures of Augie March,*
    56
Dostoyevsky, Fyodor
  Bellow in tradition of,
    2–3
  influence on Bellow, 16
  influence seen in *The
    Victim,* 28–29
Dreiser, Theodore
  *The Adventures of Augie
    March* in tradition of,
    48
  Bellow and, 3
  influence on *The Victim,*
    28

Einhorn, William, *see*
  William Einhorn
Eliot, T. S.
  the "wasteland" metaphor,
    16
Ellison, Ralph, 84
  the "invisible man" meta-
    phor, 15–16
"Eternal Husband, The"
  (Dostoyevsky)
  The Victim compared to,
    28–29
existential concerns, Bellow
  characters and, *see
  also* reality
  being versus *becoming,* 55,
    80, 82, 89, 107, 128
  defiance of philosophical
    pessimism, 92, 97–98,
    99–100, 100–101
  definition of man, 26, 27,
    28, 49–50, 118
  fear of annihilation, 16,
    75, 80, 82, 83, 85–86
  identity, problems of, *see*
    identity

standard of conduct,
  search for, 3, 13, 27–
  28, 33, 79–80, 118
worthwhile fate, search
  for, 33–34, 37–38, 39–
  40, 41, 44, 46

"Father-to-be, A," 71, 72
Faulkner, William, 80
  Bellow and, 2, 3
Fenchel, Thea, *see* Thea
  Fenchel
Fielding, Henry
  *The Adventures of Augie
    March* and, 57
Fitzgerald, F. Scott
  Bellow and, 3
Flaubert, Gustave
  influence on *The Victim,*
    28

"Gonzaga Manuscripts,
  The," 71
Grandma Lausch, 33–56

Hamlet (Shakespeare)
  *The Adventures of Augie
    March* passages com-
    pared to, 49
Harper, Gordon, 17, 28, 29
Hassan, Ihab, 34
Hawthorne, Nathaniel
  Bellow in tradition of, 2–3
Hemingway, Ernest, 79
  *The Adventures of Augie
    March* in tradition of,
    48
  Bellow and, 3
Henderson, 41, 50, 55, 78–
  89, 94, 108, 111, 113,
  114
  Bellow and, 88
  violence in the nature of,
    80, 81

Henderson the Rain King,
38, 41, 44, 75, 78–89,
94, 113, 127
quoted, 87, 88
Herzog, 2, 29, 44, 74, 75,
92–111, 113, 120, 126,
127
as *Bildungsroman,* 102–
103
as the end of a develop-
ment, 92
as a novel of ideas, 94, 97,
98–104
quoted, 98–100, 107, 109,
110
Herzog, Moses, *see* Moses
Herzog

ideas
importance and function
of, *see* Bellow; novel
of ideas
environment of, *see*
themes
identity, problems of, in Bellow characters, *see also*
existential concerns;
reality
affirmation of a common
humanity, 11, 15, 18,
22–24, 25, 26, 46, 70,
85–86, 100, 101, 108–
109, 114
assertion of individuality,
35 (*see also* Augie
March, quality of
opposition)
efforts to establish, 16, 17,
38, 67–68
relation to objects, 13–14,
27, 47, 70, 86, 87, 108
imagination, powers of, *see*
Bellow; themes
interior monologue

Bellow's use of, 75
Invisible Man (Ellison)
as metaphor, 15–16
Henderson the Rain King
and, 84
irony
in *The Adventures of
Augie March,* 44, 47,
51–52
in *Dangling Man,* 15
in *Mr. Sammler's Planet,*
120
in *Seize the Day,* 66
in *The Victim,* 28

James, Henry, 71
influence on *The Victim,*
28
Jewish influence
in *Herzog,* 92, 94
on Bellow, 5, 93–94
Joseph, 8–17, 68
Joyce, James
Bellow and, 3

Kafka, Franz
Bellow in tradition of, 2–3
King Dahfu, 78–89
Kirby Allbee, 17–28
as Everyman, 20, 26

Last Analysis, The, 111–15
first performance of, 114
Lausch, Grandma, *see*
Grandma Lausch
Lawrence, D. H.
Bellow and, 3
Lazarillo de Tormes
Augie March and, 57
"Leaving the Yellow
House," 74
Lessing, Doris, 80
Leventhal, Asa, *see* Asa
Leventhal

"Life among the Machiavellians," *see The Adventures of Augie March*
"Looking for Mr. Green," 71–72

Madeleine Pontritter, 72, 92–111, 113
Mailer, Norman, 57, 80
    quoted, 2
Malraux, André
    "condition humaine" metaphor, 16
March, Augie, *see* Augie March
March, Simon, *see* Simon March
Melville, Herman
    The Adventures of Augie March in tradition of, 48
    Bellow in tradition of, 2–3
metaphors in Bellow works, 15–16, 42, 67, 69, 100, 106, 113, 118
"Mexican General, The," 64, 74
Mr. Sammler, *see* Artur Sammler
Mr. Sammler's Planet, 60, 62, 118–26, 127
    quoted, 121
Mosby's Memoirs (collection), 24, 74, 75
"Mosby's Memoirs" (short story), 74
Moses Herzog, 46, 72, 74, 92–111, 113, 114, 115, 122
    Bellow and, 93

Nabokov, Vladimir
    Bellow in tradition of, 54

narrative perspectives, *see* style and technique
National Book Award for Fiction, ix, x, 4
Notes from Underground (Dostoyevsky), 16
novel, the
    Bellow's attitudes toward, 5–6, 56–57, 75, 102, 126–27, 128
novel of ideas
    Bellow and, 127
    Herzog as, 94, 97, 98–104
    The Victim as, 17–18

"Old System, The," 74
Order, idea of, in Bellow's works, *see* themes

Paris Review, 28
Philip Bummidge, 111–15, 127
Pontritter, Madeleine, *see* Madeleine Pontritter
Proust, Marcel
    Bellow in tradition of, 54
Pychon, Thomas, 57

realism in Bellow's works, 2
reality, *see also* existential concerns; identity
    longing for, 58
    necessity for new attitude toward, 13, 100
    possibilities of, 44, 68, 86, 111, 113–14, 121
    reality "constructors" (reality "instructors"), 39–40, 43–44, 45–46, 64, 109, 110–11, 121
Russian writers, nineteenth-century
    Bellow and, 3

Sammler, Mr. Artur, *see* Artur Sammler
Sartre, Jean-Paul
Bellow in tradition of, 2–3
influence on *The Victim*, 28
Saul Bellow: In Defense of Man (Clayton), 2
Schlossberg, 17–28, 41, 79
Scott, Nathan, 2
Seize the Day, 8, 17, 44, 60, 62–71, 75, 101
quoted, 65, 66–67, 69, 70
"Sermon by Doctor Pep," 49
Simon March, 33–56, 80
Simplicius Simplicissimus
Augie March and, 57
Smollett, Tobias
The Adventures of Augie March and, 57
"Some Notes on Recent American Fiction," 79
Stella, 33–56
Sterne, Laurence
The Adventures of Augie March and, 57
style and technique in Bellow's writing
ambiguous endings, 8, 21–22, 68–69
form, restrained versus unrestrained, 60, 62, 70–71
general, 6, 17, 34, 35, 55–56, 60, 102, 125, 126, 127–28
interior monologue, 75
the mind as "setting," 74
narrative perspective, 62, 84, 95–96, 111
picaresque elements, 34, 35, 57, 78
satire, 86, 88

significant change in, 29, 34, 56–57
symbols in Bellow novels, 67, 73, 78–79

Tamkin, Dr., *see* Dr. Tamkin
technique, *see* style and technique
Thea Fenchel, 33–56
themes in Bellow works
dangers of abundance, 47–48
existential concerns, *see* individual entry
identity, *see* individual entry
imagination, powers of, 86–88, 94, 125
money as symbol of corruption, 71, 72–73
order, man's need for, 5–6, 17, 60–62, 94–95, 124, 125–26
reality, *see* individual entry
survival in environment of ideas, 73, 112–13, 114, 127
the "victim," 13, 20, 28, 62–63, 105–106
Thousand and One Nights
quoted in *The Victim*, 18
Tommy Wilhelm, 62–71, 127
"Trip to Galena, The," 32–33, 74
quoted, 33
Tu As Raison Aussi, *see* Joseph
Twain, Mark
Bellow in tradition of, 2–3
"Two Morning Monologues," 4, 16, 74

victim, the, in Bellow's
        works, 13, 20, 62–63
        (*see also* themes)
Victim, The, 8, 17–28, 29, 41,
        56–57, 60, 62, 65
    quoted, 22–23, 24, 25, 26,
        27
"victim literature," 28, 105–
        106

Warren, Robert Penn
    Bellow in tradition of, 2–3
Wen, A, 73
"Where Do We Go from
        Here: The Future of
        Fiction," 102
Whitman, Walt
    *The Adventures of Augie
        March* in tradition of,
        48

Bellow and, 3
Why Are We in Vietnam?
        (Mailer)
    Henderson the Rain King
        and, 80
Wilhelm, Tommy, *see*
        Tommy Wilhelm
Wilhelm Meister (Goethe)
    *The Adventures of Augie
        March* compared to,
        57
William Einhorn, 33–56
W.P.A. writer's project, 4
Wrecker, The, 71, 72–73
"Writer as Moralist, The,"
        101–102
Wurlitzer, Rudolph, 57

Yeats, William Butler
    Bellow and, 3

DATE DUE

11/16			
FEB 7 1973			
AUG 1 5 1973			
DEC 3 10:30			
DEC 8 4.5			
DEC 8 2:30			
DEC 9			
DEC 9 5:15			
DEC 9			
EC 10 5.45			
DEC 10			
DEC 11			
DEC 12			
DEC 12			
DEC 14			
MY 15			
GAYLORD			PRINTED IN U.S.A